P9-AFR-546

AARP Facebook
Tech to Connect®

This Large Print Book carries the
Seal of Approval of N.A.V.H.

AARP Facebook Tech to Connect®

Marsha Collier

THORNDIKE PRESS
A part of Gale, Cengage Learning

Detroit • New York • San Francisco • New Haven, Conn • Waterville, Maine • London

Copyright © 2012 by John Wiley & Sons, Inc.

Thorndike Press, a part of Gale, Cengage Learning.

ALL RIGHTS RESERVED

Trademarks: Wiley, the Wiley logo, and For Dummies are trademarks or registered trademarks of John & Sons, Inc. and/or its affiliates in the United States and other countries, and may not be used without written permission. AARP and the AARP logo are registered trademarks of AARP. Facebook is a registered trademark of Facebook, Inc. All other trademarks are the property of their respective owners. John Wiley & Sons, Inc. is not associated with any product or vendor mentioned in this book.

LIMIT OF LIABILITY/DISCLAIMER OF WARRANTY: THE PUBLISHER, AARP, AND THE AUTHOR MAKE NO REPRESENTATIONS OR WARRANTIES WITH RESPECT TO THE ACCURACY OR COMPLETENESS OF THE CONTENTS OF THIS WORK AND SPECIFICALLY DISCLAIM ALL WARRANTIES, INCLUDING WITHOUT LIMITATION WARRANTIES OF FITNESS FOR A PARTICULAR PURPOSE. NO WARRANTY MAY BE CREATED OR EXTENDED BY SALES OR PROMOTIONAL MATERIALS. THE ADVICE AND STRATEGIES CONTAINED HEREIN MAY NOT BE SUITABLE FOR EVERY SITUATION. THIS WORK IS SOLD WITH THE UNDERSTANDING THAT THE PUBLISHER AND AARP ARE NOT ENGAGED IN RENDERING LEGAL, ACCOUNTING, OR OTHER PROFESSIONAL SERVICES. IF PROFESSIONAL ASSISTANCE IS REQUIRED, THE SERVICES OF A COMPETENT PROFESSIONAL PERSON SHOULD BE SOUGHT. AARP, THE PUBLISHER, AND THE AUTHOR SHALL NOT BE LIABLE FOR DAMAGES ARISING HEREFROM. THE FACT THAT AN ORGANIZATION OR WEBSITE IS REFERRED TO IN THIS WORK AS A CITATION AND/OR A POTENTIAL SOURCE OF FURTHER INFORMATION DOES NOT MEAN THAT THE AUTHOR, AARP, OR THE PUBLISHER ENDORSES THE INFORMATION THE ORGANIZATION OR WEBSITE MAY PROVIDE OR RECOMMENDATIONS IT MAYMAKE. FURTHER, READERS SHOULD BE AWARE THAT INTERNET WEBSITES LISTED IN THIS WORK MAY HAVE CHANGED OR DISAPPEARED BETWEEN WHEN THIS WORK WAS WRITTEN AND WHEN IT IS READ.

Thorndike Press® Large Print Health, Home & Learning.

The text of this Large Print edition is unabridged.

Other aspects of the book may vary from the original edition.

Set in 16 pt. Plantin.

LIBRARY OF CONGRESS CATALOGING-IN-PUBLICATION DATA

Collier, Marsha.
  AARP Facebook : tech to connect / by Marsha Collier. — Large print edition.
    pages cm. — (Thorndike Press large print health, home & learning)
   ISBN-13: 978-1-4104-5501-7 (hardcover)
   ISBN-10: 1-4104-5501-7 (hardcover)
   1. Facebook (Electronic resource) 2. Online social networks. 3. Social media. 4. Internet and older people. I. Title.
  HM743.F33C64 2013
  004.67'80846—dc23

               2012050727

Published in 2013 by arrangement with John Wiley & Sons, Inc.

Printed in Mexico
1 2 3 4 5 6 7 17 16 15 14 13

Connections that work for you

More than 60 percent of adults use Facebook regularly, and the 55-and-older crowd is the fastest-growing group on the site. That's no surprise: We're all using this social network to connect — finding old friends and meeting new ones, sharing photos and videos with kids and grandkids, and learning new things. Whether you're intimidated and afraid that it's too late to start — or you just need a little help with all the icons and lingo — this book is for you.

Dedicated to helping you stay connected with friends, family, and community, AARP has teamed up with the Dummies brand to offer sound advice and solutions for using *tech to connect*. This easy-to-understand resource offers the following:

■ The basics of social networking with Facebook, and why you need to get on board.

■ Step-by-step instructions for doing everything from posting to sharing photos to playing games — all free!

- Ways to protect your security, including sending private messages and blocking specific people.

So welcome to this new universe. Let us be your guide.

AARP

AARP is a nonprofit, nonpartisan membership organization that helps people 50 and older improve their lives. For more than 50 years, AARP has been serving our members and society by creating positive social change. AARP's mission is to enhance the quality of life for all as we age; lead positive social change; and deliver value to members through information, service and advocacy.

Dedications

To all the future online citizens who have purchased this book to get a taste of how much fun joining the online party can be. I look forward to seeing you on Facebook, hearing your stories, and learning from you.

I dedicate this book also to my dear friends on Facebook who have embraced me as part of the community. I want to thank all of you for your help and support; you make the online world a fun place to visit for millions of people. Keep on doing what you're doing.

Author's Acknowledgments

This book couldn't have been written without the input from the thousands of wonderful people I've met online from all over the world. You inspire me to work harder and do my best to help as many people as possible.

I particularly want to thank my freaking brilliant editors at John Wiley & Sons, Inc. who helped make this book as much fun as it is: my über-smart (and charming) project editor Leah Michael; my super-funny editor Barry Childs-Helton; my tech editor TJ McCue; my acquisitions editor Steven Hayes, who is always there for support and ideas; and my publisher Andy Cummings.

Thank you all!

Publisher's Acknowledgments

We're proud of this book; please send us your comments at http://dummies.custhelp.com. For other comments, please contact our Customer Care Department within the U.S. at 877-762-2974, outside the U.S. at 317-572-3993, or fax 317-572-4002.

Some of the people who helped bring this book to market include the following:

Acquisitions and Editorial

Senior Editorial Manager: Leah Michael

Executive Editor: Steven Hayes

Senior Copy Editor: Barry Childs-Helton

Technical Editor: TJ McCue

Editorial Assistant: Amanda Graham

Sr. Editorial Assistant: Cherie Case

Cover Photo: ©iStockphoto.com/Alex Branwell; ©iStockphoto.com/YinYang

Special Help: Katie Mohr

Composition Services for the Original Edition

Project Coordinator: Kristie Rees

Layout and Graphics: Melissa Auciello-Brogan, Sennett Vaughan Johnson, Jennifer Mayberry, Erin Zeltner

Proofreaders: Lindsay Amones, Debbye Butler

Indexer: BIM Indexing & Proofreading Services

Publishing and Editorial for Technology Dummies

Richard Swadley, Vice President and Executive Group Publisher

Andy Cummings, Vice President and Publisher

Mary Bednarek, Executive Acquisitions Director

Mary C. Corder, Editorial Director

Publishing for Consumer Dummies

Kathleen Nebenhaus, Vice President and Executive Publisher

Composition Services

Debbie Stailey, Director of Composition Services

Contents at a Glance

Table of Contents

Introduction

Sometimes the fear of climbing a mountain can be overcome with a single step. Not for me — I wouldn't climb a mountain at any age, but I just might take a baby step and make my way (unwittingly) upward as I observe the plants and enjoy the view. Who knows? Before I know it, I may be halfway up the mountain.

Look at new technology (such as Facebook) as that mountain. See the benefits and enjoy the view. Don't miss the opportunity to join your friends and family in this new world just because it may be . . . a little scary. I was a little scared the first time I tasted jalapeno jelly and, although I could have lived without the experience, I thought it worthwhile to give it a try. Life is like that. You never know if you're going to like that bon-bon unless you at least give it a bite (and I hate missing out on the butterscotch-filled ones).

An important thing to keep in mind is that the Internet is an ever-changing place. Pages look different in various browsers, and the smart kids behind Facebook are constantly tinkering with the site to make it more user-friendly. So, as you read this introduction (and this book), realize that the Facebook pages you see onscreen may not look exactly the same as the images I see — and the order in the steps may change. But what's here will give you a good strong start on the path to mastering the mysteries of Facebook — and might just get you all the way there.

About This Book

This book exists because we have all sorts of new technologies within reach, but their complexity may keep us from diving in. Facebook gives us the power to connect with friends from the past, far-flung family members, and coworkers. That's not all. When utilized with the activities in this book, it can open new horizons by giving you new ways to meet new people and learn new things.

In my experiences on Facebook, I've joined Groups and learned about new hobbies. I've encountered amiable strangers — who are now no longer strangers — who have helped me get better at understanding a plethora of subjects. Not to mention new growth in familiar interests: My knitting skills (for example) are no longer limited to "knit one, purl two," thanks to a lovely lady in Seattle who introduced me to a new community that taught me how to follow patterns and actually have something worthwhile after I've spent hours knitting.

Facebook is the community of the technology world, bringing together people from around the world who have similar interests and ideas. We can sit at home wearing whatever we wish and communicate with old and new friends. We can also use Facebook to connect with opportunities for involvement in community events, political discussions, and other activities that keep our lives vibrant.

Just today I used Facebook for a good reason: I spoke to my daughter yesterday — it seemed like she was having a bad day. Like a good mom, I didn't want to bug her at work to see how she was doing. So I went to her Facebook Page — and saw that her post this morning was very positive. Without intruding into her life, I felt better because she did. That sort of thing happens all the time.

Part of the etiquette — when peering into the lives of our friends and family — is that we can look, observe, and comment occasionally, but we have to remember it's public. Know that whatever we chose to say to (or about) these folks on their Facebook Pages can be seen by all *their* friends. Facebook is for observing, dropping in now and then, and maybe providing a little evidence that someone cares — not critiquing in public. In addition, a word to the wise: The information you glean from visiting friends and family online is best kept close to the chest. A little common courtesy in this new world can spare you the risk of being too limited in your view of loved ones.

Who This Book Is For

This book is for you. Because you were inquisitive enough to open the cover and peer inside, I know you have an interest in social media and want to know more. I've written this book in plain terms, the way I prefer to be taught something (I don't like having to wade through techno-speak — and I don't like being talked down to).

It's written to open the doors for all the intuitive minds who might feel like technology rushes faster than a tsunami and don't want to be left behind. Here's your chance to get pleasantly immersed and fall in love (fall in Like?) with one of the newest modes of communication for the 21st century. If you have concerns about your safety and privacy in this social media world, you'll be happy to know that this book explains how to establish settings that help safeguard your Facebook information. And if you're already active on Facebook, you can use this book to delve deeper into everything that the Facebook platform offers.

We've been through a lot in the past decades. We're pretty lucky to have been able to learn lessons and now to live by them. We know cause and effect; every action has an equal reaction. Diving into the online space is an expansion of the experiences we already have had. It can only serve to enhance our continued time on the planet.

Conventions

Nope, no name tags or secret handshakes required. The conventions in this book are there to help you see the varied twists and turns.

- I try to capitalize titles of new places you visit online and italicize items that need definition, so you can match the written word to what you see on your screen and recognize a new feature or concept.

- When a link is involved — meaning there is a new place online that you need to visit — I put in the URL (Internet address) so you can type it directly into your browser.

- Often there's more than one way to accomplish something. I try to give you all the options I can discover — just in case Facebook chooses to change things in the future. You'll be able to find your way (one way or the other).

- Tips. Love 'em. This is where, if you and I were sitting next to each other, I'd tap you on the shoulder to interject something that I think you need to know — a nugget of info that will enhance or explain the how and why of doing something. Consider these my personal messages to you.

- Sidebars. Think of these as expanded tips. My editor suggests that if my tips get long-winded, I can just write a sidebar to explain further — so now and then I do. I also use sidebars to give you further insights into the topic at hand.

■ Figures. I used my own Facebook account for this book so you could see Pages that are deeply involved in the various areas of Facebook. I'm sure my online friends will enjoy the fact that they are part and parcel of your education.

How This Book Is Organized

I unveil the chapters on a need-to-know basis. Going from the basic steps of signing up to the more advanced areas of Facebook — like doing video chats. Since I'm a big believer in those baby steps, I don't want to overwhelm you with the tough stuff first.

Here's a quick chapter-by-chapter run-through of what you're going to learn:

1. **Signing Up and Starting Up on Facebook.** Here you learn how to sign up and build your initial space on Facebook without looking like a newbie (hey, everybody's got to start somewhere . . . discreetly . . .). You have step-by-step instructions on how to build your initial profile (and how to go back and make changes).

2. **Finding and Making Friends: Old and New.** Hopefully, you have friends already on Facebook. *Friending* the people who become your online friends is the first step into becoming integrated into the thread of Facebook. Here I show you how to find old friends, old acquaintances, past (and current) coworkers, and family members. You also learn how to organize your groups to make life online a lot easier.

3. **Friendly Interactions.** So how do you converse with folks on Facebook? This chapter gives you the lowdown on the basics of Facebook communications. It gives you insights into the right and wrong ways (there's a little etiquette involved — manners matter, even online).

4. **Adding Photos and Videos to Your Timeline.** Part of the fun of the online world is the visual. Sharing photos and videos (even those you didn't create yourself) with friends and family gives your community insights into what you're doing and your interests. It's fun — and best of all, it's not difficult once you've read these tips.

5. **Fine-Tuning: Account and Privacy Settings.** We're all concerned with privacy. Experience tells us that once you've announced something in public, it's no longer private. Here I tell you how to limit some comments and posts to a select group of your friends — or to the entire world. It's all up to you. I give you the instructions that will allow you to post on Facebook while feeling comfortable that what you are sharing is just how you'd planned.

6. **Facebook Timeline — Your Virtual Scrapbook.** The Facebook profile page is now a Timeline. A Timeline of your life. You can be as upfront about your experiences as you wish (or not). But think how wonderful an online scrapbook of your life will be for your children. I wish my Mom had had a Facebook Timeline. What fun it would have been to have a permanent record to share with friends and members of the family.

7. **More Conversations via Pages and Groups.** Joining Groups and visiting pages is part of the fun. (It's also

a great way to get coupons from brands you follow.) By involving yourself in Groups, you'll meet — and learn from — people you'd never know otherwise.

8. **Embracing Events, Messaging, and Birthdays.** No longer do you have to buy a card and go to the post office. Facebook helps you arrange events and send birthday greetings. Never forget a birthday or anniversary again! Your communications can be even more personal via Facebook.

9. **Playing Around with Facebook Games and Apps.** Playing around . . . hmmm . . . it's more like "having fun with friends online." Communication with friends is just the tip of the iceberg on Facebook. Programs called *apps* are available to get you started playing virtual board games — or thousands of other games. You'll also learn how to video-chat with your friends and family — that's gold! (And very futuristic, except now it's real.)

Chapter 1

Signing Up and Starting Up on Facebook

It seems that the kids are always having all the fun, right? They're certainly all over the nooks and crannies of Facebook, and treat it like it's their own private playground. If the kids can master the secret sauces of this online social hangout, surely we — who have attained a level of wisdom and adaptability — can get in there and benefit from all

tech 2 connect

activities

- Registering Your Profile
- Building Your Profile
- Setting Your Profile Information's Privacy Level
- Adding More about You

29

the extra features, too! Facebook just might become the first stop you make as you start each day (maybe while you drink your coffee in the morning?). It has become mine.

Before you can take a baby step into this Brave New World of Facebook, you need to fill out a bit of online paperwork. Just as in so many life experiences, the fine print can make or break a pleasant event. In this chapter, I show you how to register on Facebook, build your Profile, and set up your Account and Privacy settings so that you'll feel safer and more at home online with your Facebook friends.

Registering Your Profile

After you start your computer, open your Internet browser. Depending on your computer or your personal preferences, you may have Internet Explorer, Firefox, Chrome, or Safari aboard. Fire it up and follow these steps:

1. Type www.facebook.com in the URL area. A web page will appear, looking something like the page in Figure 1-1 — a portal to a whole new world of fun!

   URL stands for *Uniform Resource Locator*, the global address of documents and pages on the Internet.

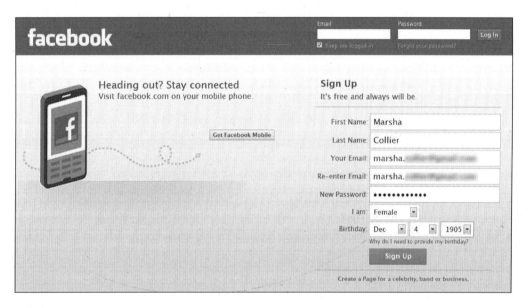

Figure 1-1

2. Type your name in the appropriate boxes. Type your first name in the box labeled *First Name* and your last name in the other box. I advise that you use your real

name because you are joining Facebook to meet up with your friends, right? Your coworkers may never find you if you use your grade-school moniker (if you're a bit more reserved these days, do you *want* everybody to know your nickname was something like Skippy?).

3. Type your preferred e-mail address, and do it once again. Typing your e-mail address a second time helps ensure that you submit the right e-mail address. If you type in two different e-mail addresses, Facebook will ask you to correct your error. And if your typing is anything like mine, errors do occur.

I say *preferred* e-mail address because you might want to set up an e-mail account just for your Facebook interactions. Having a separate account accomplishes two things: It keeps your personal e-mail address private and relates only your Facebook e-mail address to your doings on Facebook.

4. Think up a good, secure password and type it in the box where prompted. You won't see the characters as you type them, so I recommend being extra careful with your keystrokes. Be sure you remember your password (perhaps write it down and keep the paper in a secret place?). See the sidebar "Selecting a good password" for some good tips on picking a secure, easy-to-remember password.

5. Indicate your sex (this is required, not an option). Click on the small arrow beside the box next to *I am:* and a drop-down menu will appear with your options.

6. Try to remember your birthdate and fill it in using the drop-down menus. I say *try* to remember because I

generally forget my birth year (I always remember the month and day). I also admit that when I registered on Facebook, I put my birth year as 1981 (my little way of not revealing my true age). It's important to put in your correct birth month and day, because Facebook puts you on the birthday list for that day — and you want to be able to enjoy all those greetings your friends will no doubt post to your Page.

Don't worry; Facebook doesn't check on how old you really are. But always remember what birth year you give any website (1966 sounds like a good year, eh?). That's because if you forget your password sometime down the road, the site may ask for your birth year as confirmation that you are really you. In the section "Setting Your Profile Information's Privacy Level" later in this chapter, I show you how to hide your birth year (should you decide to post it) from other Facebook users.

7. Check your work in the boxes you've just filled out and, if all is well, click Sign Up. You will be sent to a new page.

At this point, Facebook will send you a couple of e-mail messages. One message confirms that you have given Facebook a legitimate contact e-mail address. It includes a clickable link, which will enable you to broaden your Facebook experience. You need to respond to this e-mail because you can't get complete control of your account unless Facebook knows it's really you (a person, not a computer robot) opening an account. You will also get an additional e-mail prompting you to add friends from your e-mail and contacts lists.

Selecting a good password

Poorly chosen passwords are the number-one loophole for hackers. Any password can be cracked by the right person in a matter of seconds. Your goal is to set a password that takes too much of the hackers' time. With the number of available users on Facebook, odds are they'll go to the next potential victim's password rather than spend too many minutes (or even hours) trying to crack yours.

Here are some industrial-strength tips for setting a secure password.

- Watch the number of characters: Compose your password of more than eight characters.

- Use case sensitivity: Since passwords are case-sensitive, take advantage of the feature. Mix lower- and uppercase in your passwords.

- Use letters, symbols, and numbers: Combine letters, symbols, and numbers to make your passwords harder to crack.

- Avoid proper words: Don't use proper words; if the word appears in a dictionary — any dictionary — it's easy for a computer to look up in almost no time. Instead, think of the title of your favorite book. Make your password the first two letters of each word in that title, with numbers in the middle (not sequential).

- Avoid the obvious: A painfully obvious example is the word *password.* D'oh!

- Avoid birthdays: Don't use your birthday, your friend's birthday, or John F. Kennedy's birthday. Not only are these dates common knowledge, but so is this truism: A series of numbers is easy to crack.

- Avoid names: Don't use your first or last name, your dog's name, or anyone's name. Again, it's common knowledge and easy to find out. (Most people know my ex-husband's name; it's been in many of my books!)

- Avoid contact numbers: Social Security Number (if anyone gets hold of that one — watch out!), phone numbers, your e-mail address, or street address (got a White Pages? So do the con artists . . .).

- Avoid any of the lousy passwords in Table 1-1: These have been gleaned from the millions of password dictionaries available from hackers. Note that this is not a complete list by any means; there are thousands of common (lousy) passwords, and unprintable ones are more common than you may think. If you really care to scare yourself, Google the phrase "common passwords."

As a matter of security? Consider doing what I do: I generally never click links in e-mail. I go back to my browser and log on to Facebook when I want to visit my friends online. You can always add your friends after you log in to the Facebook site. But in the case of the Facebook verification e-mail, you should go ahead and click the link — especially if you just started the sign-up process. You know that you requested this communication!

Table 1-1	**Easily Cracked and Most Frequently Used Passwords**			
!@#$%	!@#$%^&	!@#$%^&*(	0	0000
00000000	0007	007	01234	123456
02468	24680	1	1101	111
11111	111111	1234	12345	1234qwer
123abc	123go	12	131313	212
310	2003	2004	54321	654321
888888	a	aaa	abc	abc123
action	absolut	access	admin	admin123
jesus	administrator	alpha	asdf	animal
yourfirstname	computer	beatles	enable	fubar
home	internet	login	letmein	mypass
mypc	owner	pass	password	passwrd
papa	peace	penny	grace	qwerty
secret	sunshine	temp	temp123	test
test123	whatever	whatnot	winter	windows
xp	xxx	yoda	mypc123	sexy

8. Type the words you see on the page (they're usually distorted) into the text box — and, again, click the Sign Up button. Figure 1-2 shows you an instance of such a *captcha code* — a barely recognizable alphabetic or numeric code. It's presented as a picture, not as text, to determine whether you can read the words or numbers and *then* type them in. A human being can do that; a computer that's trying to set up fake Facebook accounts can't (at least not yet). Correctly typing a captcha code is a test that humans — but not computers — can pass. Once you've typed in the words, click the Sign Up button. When you do, you're taken to another page.

Fortunately, if the captcha code is such a mess that you can't read it, you can click the Try Different Words link to load a different set of words. If all else fails, be sure your speakers are on (they usually are) and click the An Audio Captcha link: Then the captcha words are read aloud to you through your computer's speakers.

Sign Up

It's free and always will be.

Security Check

Enter both words below, separated by a space.
Can't read the words below? Try different words or an audio captcha.

oefiexia (Jenny

Text in the box: [   ]   What's this?

◄ Back   **Sign Up**

By clicking Sign Up, you are indicating that you have read and agree to the Terms of Use and Privacy Policy.

Figure 1-2

9. Finding Friends is the next step, as pictured in Figure 1-3. At this point in the process, Facebook encourages you to enter your e-mail address so an automatic search of your e-mail can suggest friends of yours who are currently on Facebook. If you are comfortable doing this, be my guest — but I recommend you click the link that says *Skip this step* (at bottom-right onscreen) until you've set up your page so you feel more at ease when you reach out to others.

You can always visit this friend-finding activity later. For now, I suggest that you just concentrate on filling out the cyber-paperwork to build your Profile.

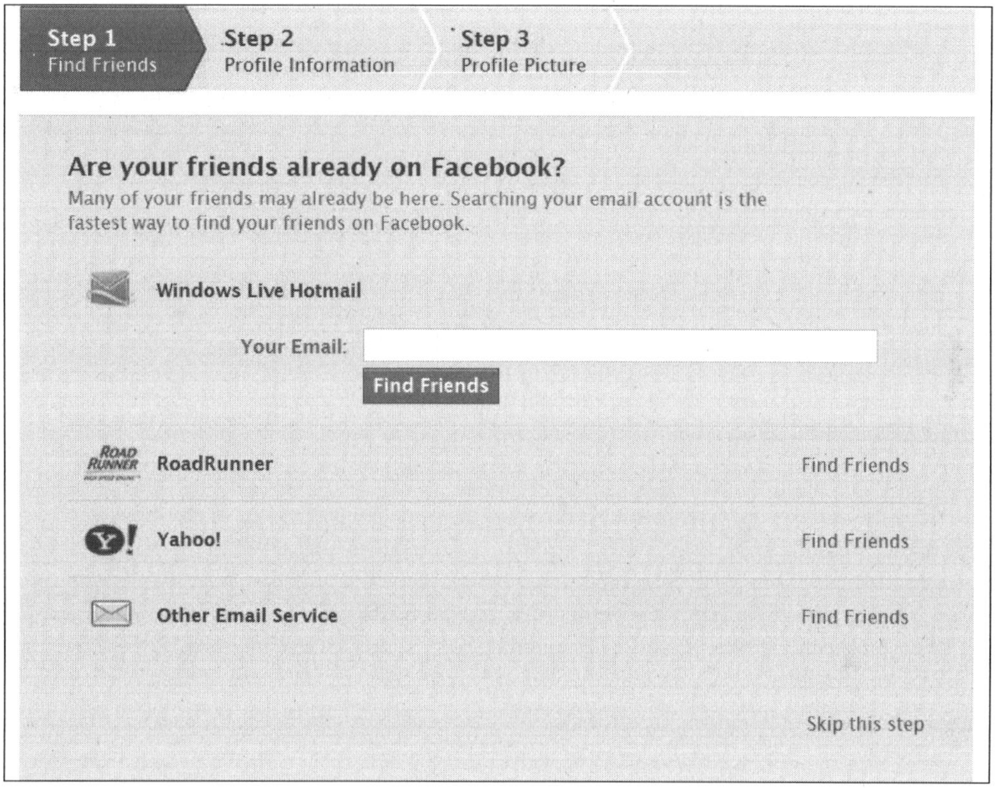

Figure 1-3

Building Your Profile

Your Profile on Facebook may very well be your first authorized, official profile online. Through your profiles, you let people (friends, coworkers, and relations) know about you and what is going on in your life. For example, profiles commonly include information about your interests (TV, books, and movies), politics, work history, and your family — whatever you feel comfortable sharing. Type in your favorite books, movies, and TV shows to get links to a page where you can meet others who have similar likes. Facebook is all about connecting with people, and this is the best place to start.

Don't feel daunted here; you can change your Facebook Profile information at any time. You can add, delete, or change information as you wish.

Filling out the suggested information is completely optional, and you can click Skip at any point in the beginning process. You can always come back and fill in dates and other details later (but only if you wish).

1. Enter your High School, College/University, and Past Employers. Facebook content gets really personal at this point, asking you to enter your basic profile information, beginning with

   ■ The high school you attended and your year of graduation. When you begin to type your school name, Facebook suggests schools that match. If your school is mentioned, click it. If not, type in the name.

- ■ Your college (if any) and graduation year. If you choose to add in your schools, the graduation year is optional.

- ■ The company you work for (or worked for).

If you want to keep your age private, you don't need to choose dates from the drop-down menu. (I didn't, and Facebook let me proceed.) Of course, if you specified your graduation year(s), that's a pretty big hint about your age. But you knew that.

2. Figure 1-4 shows how the screen looks if you add your work or education history to the Profile Information page. If you want to keep this information private for now (or forever), just click the Skip link. After you fill in as much data as you're comfortable with, click Save & Continue.

After you enter the requested personal information, up pops a window with suggested friends — similar to the window you saw earlier in the sign-up process. You may want to add some or all of these suggested friends based on your school and employment life. You can choose to befriend any or all by clicking their names. Doing so will *immediately* send a friend request to them. (Be sure you want to connect *before* you click — there's no turning back.)

Step 1	Step 2	Step 3
Find Friends	Profile Information	Profile Picture

Fill out your Profile Info

This information will help you find your friends on Facebook.

High School: [   ]

College/University: [   ]

Employer: [   ]

◄ Back   Skip [Save & Continue]

Click here to skip this information.

Figure 1-4

3. Here's where Facebook asks you to post a photo of yourself as your Profile picture. Decide whether you want to upload a photo from your computer or take one now with the built-in camera (or *webcam,* if you have one) on your computer.

The picture you post here will be your main photo on your page, the one people will see first when they come looking for you. It's a good idea for this photo to be a flattering and friendly image. Don't panic! You can upload any picture to fill the void for now and then change it at any time. You *could* skip this step, but why not try this? Figure 1-5 shows you the two posting options as Facebook presents them, and the next steps examine both.

42

4. Upload a photo from your computer. Do you have a picture of yourself on your computer that you'd like to share? If so, follow the steps that start here. If you don't have a photo available, and your computer has a camera, skip down to Step 8 for those instructions.

5. Click the Choose File button to start your picture selection as shown in Figure 1-6. The File Upload window opens and a directory of your computer's contents will appear.

6. Go to the folder where you store your photos and click to select an image that you'd like to display on your Facebook Profile. Be sure your selected photo's file size is no bigger than 4 MB (megabytes). (If you don't know what that means, or can't tell how big your photo is, don't worry; Facebook will let you know if it's too large.) The name of the photo you chose should appear at the bottom of the window in the File Name text box.

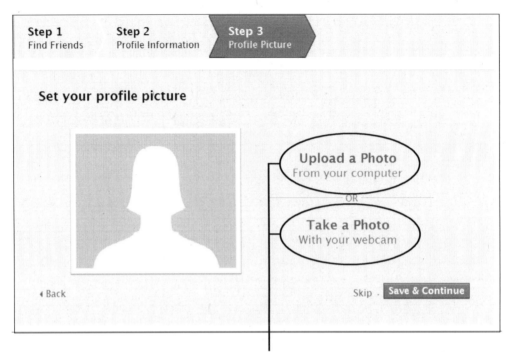

Figure 1-5

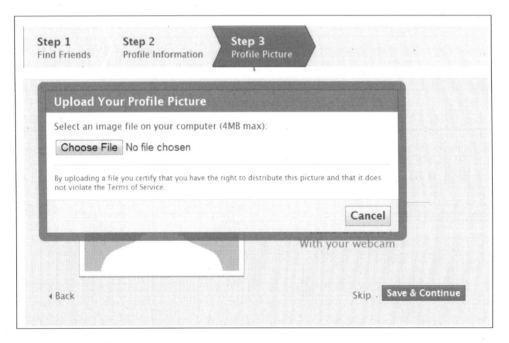

Figure 1-6

If you question whether the photo is too large, the size should be visible onscreen, next to the image name and given in kilobytes (KB) within your directory folder. If it's too big, you can preview it in Windows Photo Gallery, iPhoto, or other software and crop it to a smaller size.

Note: In this chapter, I show you figures of the screens I see on a PC that runs Windows Vista. Depending on what operating system you use on your computer, your screens may look a little different. But don't worry, the steps are the same.

7. Click Open, and the picture you chose will begin to make its merry way through the web to Facebook automatically. (Nice, huh?)

8. If you don't like the photo you selected, you can always change it later in the Edit Profile Picture area. (You can find this at the top of your Profile page.)

9. If you don't already have any photos you like, take a picture with your webcam.

   If your computer has a webcam, you can click Take a Photo with Your Webcam on the Set Your Profile Picture window (refer to Figure 1-5).

10. A window appears, as shown in Figure 1-7, asking permission for Facebook to access your camera and microphone. Select the option button next to Allow.

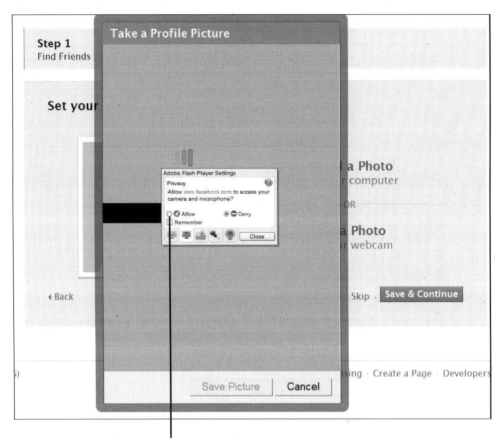

Click here to take your picture.

Figure 1-7

11. Assuming that your webcam is pointing in the right direction, you will now see your image (as you sit at your computer) in the Take a Profile Picture window. Well, you kind of see it. If you want your computer to remember that you grant access to your camera at any time to Facebook, you must click the check box next to Remember. If you don't want to grant blanket access, that's okay, too (I don't — refer to Figure 1-7). So click Close, and there you are, in all your glory.

12. You may now pose for your picture. When you're satisfied with how your picture appears, click the small

camera icon at the bottom of your image.

13. Facebook has now taken your picture! If you're happy with it (or as happy as you can be at the moment), click the Save Picture button and your photo will upload to your Facebook Profile. Remember, you can always swap out this picture later.

14. After you click Save Picture, your newly taken photo will appear on the Set Your Profile Picture page, as shown in Figure 1-8 (hmmm . . . I might have to change that photo later).

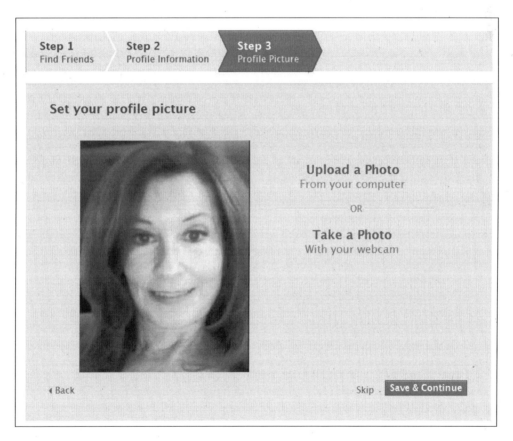

Figure 1-8

Take a breath and check your mailbox (if you haven't already) to check for your e-mail address confirmation from Facebook. Before you click the link, be sure that the e-mail (in the return address) *is* really from Facebook. Look for the line at the bottom (as shown in Figure 1-9) that says "Didn't sign up for Facebook?" next to a Please Let Us Know clickable link. Looking for minute details in an e-mail can go a long way to confirm their veracity.

Figure 1-9

A bit about Privacy settings

Facebook gives you lots of options for privacy. Setting the various options can be a chore and you might leave out a bit of information that you might want your friends to see. If some of your auld acquaintances look up your name, they may not recognize you from your picture — and if you have no further information on who you are, they may just pass you by. Your current Profile photo may not look like the way they remembered you, or your face may be too small to actually recognize you.

A lot of my personal Facebook Page is open to the public. There's nothing there that I have any problem with the world knowing. I don't get involved in (ahem) *spirited* political or religious discussions, and so try not to encourage folks who are too fond of sounding off and taking umbrage. I only accept friends who fit the profile of people I know, or fit the demographics of readers of my books.

Use your good sense on Facebook and don't block out the world; you'll be surprised at how many old friends look you up!

Setting Your Profile Information's Privacy Level

After the three basic steps in the Facebook profile-building process are complete (or skipped, depending on your choices), from your Home page (or any Facebook page), you can click your name on the right side of the blue top bar and take a look at your Profile page. From your Profile (or your Timeline) page, click the Info link in the left navigation area (or click Update Info under your Cover picture, depending on how Facebook lays out your page). Figure 1-10 shows a pretty lonely Profile page, just waiting to be spruced up.

The many links to edit your Profile.

Figure 1-10

Granted, the page in the figure looks pretty bare — but notice the many areas you can click to edit the page's content. At this point, you have a chance to put together the descriptive part of your personal profile. You decide what and how much you share: Make your profile as revealing as you like, or (for a little privacy) as vague. You can get all the privacy you want for your account in the Privacy Settings on the right side of every page. (I explain further on.)

Here's the simple way to approach this task.

1. Click the Edit Profile link (with a small pen icon next to it) at the top-left of your page. You'll see an all-in-one form with individual areas to fill in.

2. Edit the content in your Basic Information section. On this page, you'll see your name along with your gender and birthdate. Now, under the Basic Information section, you'll have an opportunity to add your city of residence, hometown (if different), languages you speak, and an area to type in a short bit about you that you'd like the world to know.

3. As you fill out each line of the page, you can set individual privacy settings for each bit of data. Figure 1-11 shows you the drop-down menu that accomplishes this (get the menu by clicking the Globe button with the down arrow). You can apply these settings whenever you post a photo, create a Wall post, or put almost anything on Facebook. These ubiquitous settings allow you to set the data to appear to other Facebook users as follows:

51

- **Public:** Using the Public setting means just that, the information is open to the public. Really not a bad option. How else will your girlfriend from PS 196 find you if she doesn't see that you went there?

- **Friends:** This information is set to be seen only by people whom you approve as friends. I really enjoy visiting friends' pages and seeing their posts, discussions, and photographs. It's almost as fun as being with them!

- **Only Me:** What's the point? Why give Facebook any information you don't want to be seen by anyone? I leave things blank rather than waste my time.

Figure 1-11

- **Custom:** Selecting this option gives you a new menu that you can use to customize some important privacy settings. Clicking on the Custom link opens a new Custom Privacy window. It allows you

52

two options — labeled *Make This Visible To* and *Hide This From* — that, in turn, give you more specific choices. You can choose to make information visible to Friends, Friends of Friends, or Specific People or Lists. And when you choose to hide information, you do so by ferreting out certain people to exclude.

- **Close Friends:** You will be able to add your friends to lists as you accept their friendships.

- **Family:** Further on, I show you how to add these relationships to your profile.

- **Acquaintances:** This extra step can be burdensome. If someone is enough of an acquaintance for you to accept as a friend, you probably won't mind if this person sees your posts. On the other hand, if you work at a company, and you don't want your boss and coworkers to see certain items, you can classify those folks as Acquaintances.

A little more about Custom Privacy

When you want in-depth control over your Facebook Profile information, you might choose to customize your Privacy Settings. This sidebar has a little more information about your custom choices. Letting Friends of Friends see your information is a good setting for whatever you want to keep out of general view. If you've befriended someone from high school (for example), someone else you went to school with can find your posts through this relationship. Someone who doesn't know any of you from Adam or Eve can't.

When you choose Specific People or Lists to share your information, you can customize even further. For example, perhaps you just want your immediate family to see certain information.

The other option is Hide This From. Choose this when you want specific people not to see certain information. If you don't want your kids to see all the photos you share with your friends from your Caribbean cruise, this is the setting you use.

Adding More about You

You'll notice, at the left side of the page shown in Figure 1-12, a list of clickable links that lead to Facebook areas where you can input as little or as much information as you want. You don't have to fill in any of it. I left some of the areas blank (Philosophy especially) when I felt that the topic was too personal to share online. But it's all up to you; Facebook is flexible that way.

Filling in your interests — for example, in the Arts and Entertainment, Sports, or Activities and Interests — allows you to connect with other people who share that common interest. Through Facebook, I found a gym buddy in my neighborhood. You might just find someone who loves knitting, baseball, dogs, or any topic you're interested in when he or she sees that same interest as part of your profile.

The idea isn't to reveal so much about yourself that you eliminate any mystery. It's simply to give others on Facebook a semi-definitive and representative picture of yourself, enough so your personality comes to the surface. You can also delay filling in this information until later if you prefer. You may decide to get the lay of the Facebook land a bit more before adding more personal information. Or you might decide never to reveal this stuff at all. It's really entirely up to you.

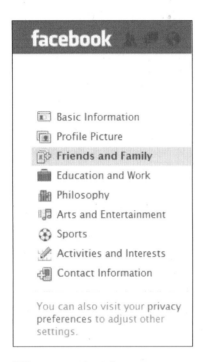

Figure 1-12

These next steps outline a few categories of information you may want to consider including.

1. Add details of your Relationship Status. Remember that you can form friendships on Facebook. My boyfriend and I first met on Facebook. If you're married, you might want to indicate so on your Profile page. Facebook is pretty open-minded when it comes to relationships; Figure 1-13 shows you the current options you can select.

   If you indicate that you're in a relationship of some sort, you then have the option of listing your anniversary date — either for others or simply to remind yourself.

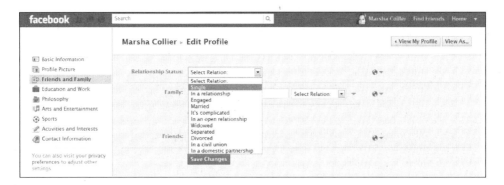

Figure 1-13

2. **Distinguish your Friends and Family.** In this area, you can connect (and announce to the world) your family members. You can still be "Friends" on Facebook with family members without indicating them as Family. But since I'm so proud of my daughter, I connected with her in this special way.

   Just type in your family member's name, and from the drop-down menu next to the text box, select the option that describes the person's relationship to you. Facebook also has many options in family relations so that no one has to feel left out. The person you name as a relative will be sent an e-mail through Facebook that asks him or her to verify that you are indeed a Relative.

3. **Offer up your Contact Information.** Click the Contact Information section, and the form in Figure 1-14 appears onscreen. Your e-mail address is already filled in because you supplied this information at the beginning of the sign-up process.

   At this point, you can type in any contact information you want your Facebook friends to see, including your

57

- *IM (instant message) screen name.* Also, you can choose the IM service you use from the associated drop-down list.

- *Mobile phone and land-line numbers.*

- *Address and zip code.*

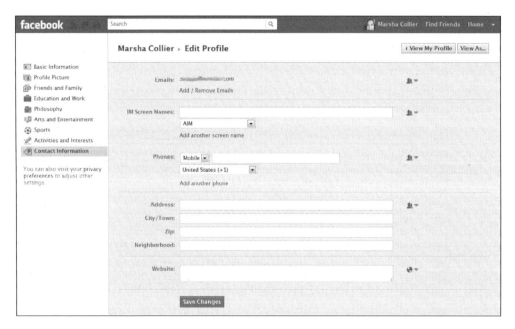

Figure 1-14

 This is where sharing too much gets sticky for me. I may make friends on Facebook whom I don't want to have my home address and phone number. For the sake of my security, I leave that part of the Facebook Profile info blank. If I want someone to have my contact information, I can always send that person an e-mail containing it.

Chapter 2

Finding and Making Friends: Old and New

Now that you've taken the first few steps and set up your Facebook Profile page, I hope you have a sense of accomplishment: You've swept by the first barrier. Now your job is to find some friends on Facebook. Think about the folks you've remembered over the years, wondering what they're doing. . . .

activities

tech **2** to connect

- Searching to Find a Friend on Facebook
- Sending a Friend Request
- Finding Friends in Other Friends' Lists
- Accepting a Friend Request
- The Navigation Bar Gets You Around
- Connecting to a Facebook Network

Start thinking back and make a list of friends from the past. Maybe start with colleagues from your previous jobs? (As I write this, I looked up my old best friend with whom I worked with in my early 20s — and yes, I think I just found her on Facebook.) Think about people from your religious group, college, high school (maybe elementary school?), Boy Scouts, Brownies, or summer camp . . . get the idea? They might just be on Facebook!

Searching to Find a Friend on Facebook

You'll be surprised that many people you know are on Facebook right now. With a little detective work, you can have a nice-size community of friends within a very short time.

I suggest you use old-fashioned paper and pen (or the word processing application on your computer) to make a list of people you'd like to find. As you think of one friend, the name of another might pop up; it's easier to keep track with a list. Once your list is started, go to Facebook and search:

1. Find the Search box at the top of any Facebook page. The Search box is part of the Navigation bar, which contains links to the important places you need to be on Facebook. (I talk about the Navigation bar in the later section "The Navigation Bar Gets You Around.")

2. Type a friend's name in the Search box, as I've done in Figure 2-1. When you're searching for anything on Facebook, a drop-down list appears — in this case, the list has semi-matching names. If you're not sure how to spell your friend's name, just type in as many characters of it as you think may be right. Facebook will pick up the slack. Alternatively, you can type in your friend's last known e-mail address. (Remember that people change e-mail addresses often these days, and it might not be valid anymore.)

Figure 2-1

3. If your friend is not on the suggested list, click the See More Results link at the bottom of the drop-down list. You'll then be sent to a page with results that match (or closely match) what you've typed in. You should be able to find your friend on this page if he or she is a member of Facebook.

4. Remember that I said you have more than one way to find friends? Type www.facebook.com/find-friends in your browser's address line.

You come to a page, Facebook's Friend Finder, as shown in Figure 2-2. Here Facebook asks that you type in your e-mail addresses and passwords (just as you did during your initial signup). Doing so will allow Facebook to import your contacts automatically. It's perfectly safe, and Facebook does not store your password.

62

Even so, I don't like it; here are some reasons why:

- I'm a stickler for privacy and do not wish to share my online contact lists with anyone.

- Friend Finder bases its automatic connections on the e-mail addresses in your address book. Facebook says,

   We may use the e-mail addresses you upload through this importer to help you connect with friends, including using this information to generate Suggestions for you and your contacts on Facebook. If you don't want us to store this information, visit this page.

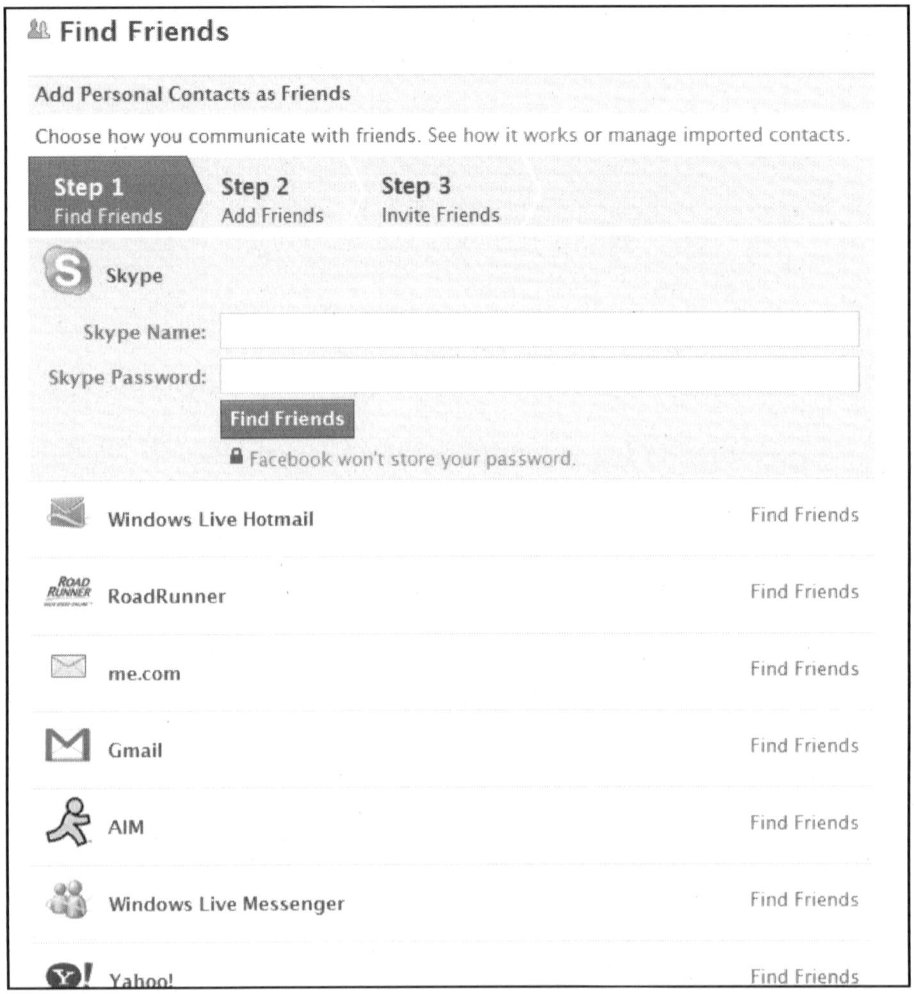

Figure 2-2

Then you have to go to that page and make your preference known.

Note: Having Facebook make suggestions for you and your e-mail contacts may sound like a fair deal. But when you click the link to read the deeper details, you're told that once you import your contacts, you must remove each one you don't want — manually, one at a time. Facebook adds a caveat: "Note that it may take some time before your name will be completely removed from Suggestions."

 If the features of Friend Finder are fine with you, feel free to add your online contact list. But be sure you read every notification you see on your screen *before* clicking and agreeing to any Facebook activity.

5. Do you remember a portion of a friend's name (say, from 20 years ago) but can't remember the rest? Perhaps a woman who has gotten married and has a new last name? Here are a couple of ways to use what you know:

■ Type www.facebook.com/srch.php in your browser to access a previous classmate or person from a company in search, as shown in Figure 2-3.

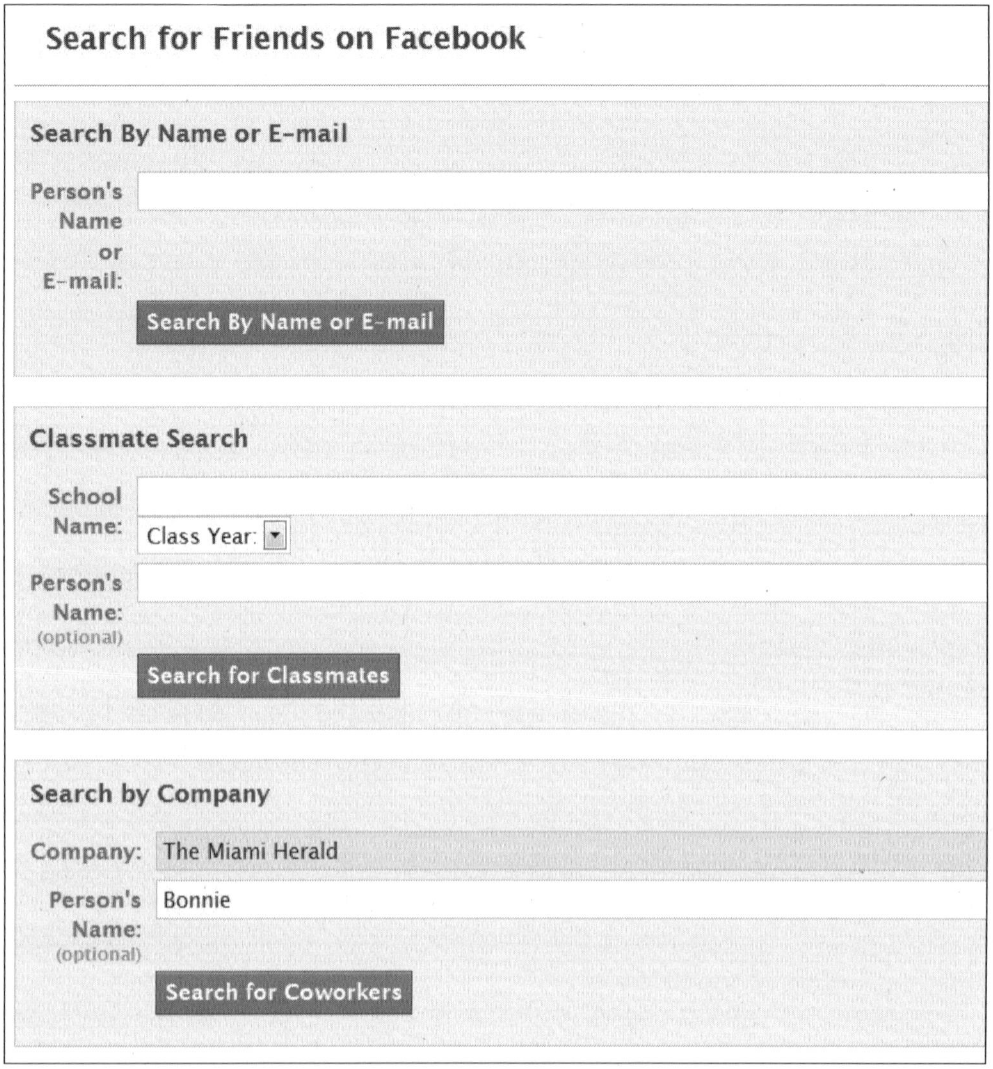

Search for Friends on Facebook

Search By Name or E-mail

Person's
Name
or
E-mail: [   ]

[Search By Name or E-mail]

Classmate Search

School
Name: [   ]

Class Year: [▾]

Person's
Name: [   ]
(optional)

[Search for Classmates]

Search by Company

Company: The Miami Herald

Person's   Bonnie
Name:
(optional)

[Search for Coworkers]

Figure 2-3

- If your friend has indicated (in his or her profile) having worked at a particular company, or having gone to a specific school or university, you can perform a search here.

- If you think your friend may have a different last name these days, you can search by first name only; if your friend used a nickname back in the day, you can search by last name.

Some folks keep their birthdates close to the chest and may not have listed on Facebook which years they attended certain schools. Try performing a search without the Class Year if you don't find your friend on the first try.

■ After you click the Search button, you'll see a page that lists people who match your search. It may take a while (Facebook has close to a billion users), but if your friends are on Facebook, you're sure to find them.

6. Another way to find a friend is to find someone you both knew together. Once you do, you can search through that person's Facebook friends. See "Finding Friends in Other Friends' Lists" later in this chapter.

Sending a Friend Request

Hopefully you've found a friend (or dozen) you'd like to connect with on Facebook. Here's where I show you how to make them official Facebook friends.

1. When you find someone on Facebook you'd like to add as a friend, doing so is a pretty simple task. After clicking the link to your prospective friend's Profile page, you will see a +1 Add Friend button next to the name.

2. Click the +1 Add Friend button and a drop-down window opens, allowing you to classify your new friend in one of your groups, as shown in Figure 2-4.

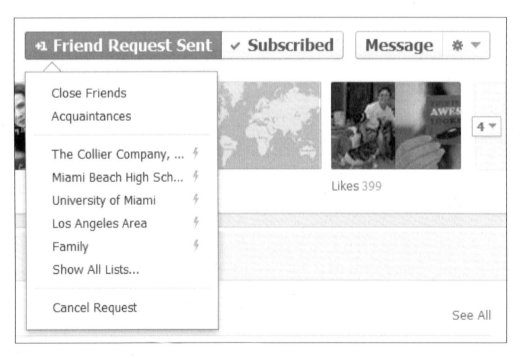

Figure 2-4

3. Your friend will now get a request through Facebook and will (with any luck) respond soon.

4. Below the +1 Add Friend (which now reads *Friend Request Sent*) is an area that may contain pictures and links to potential friends. Under the People You May Know heading are friends of your newly requested friend.

5. If you see anyone you know and would like to befriend on Facebook, click the +1 Add Friend link next to the person's picture and he or she will also receive a Friend Request.

After you send your requests, a Friend Request is posted to each recipient's Facebook notifications. Your prospective new friends also receive an e-mail notice with an easy link they can click to respond.

Finding Friends in Other Friends' Lists

Odds are that the friends you have on Facebook are connected to other people you already know. Would you like to make those people into friends on Facebook as well? It's easy. Facebook Timeline pages have Friends boxes you can find under your friends' cover photos, as shown in Figure 2-5 (unless the member has chosen to block the box from view).

A Friend box.

Figure 2-5

1. Underneath the Friends box is a friend-count number, and in the box, you see how many mutual friends you and your friend have. By clicking the Friends box, you can view all your friend's connections in a new window. A sampling of your mutual friends will appear at the top of this window (up to 12 appear, with a link to See More at the window's bottom).

   Scroll down the page; you'll find the "Friends" photos and links along with a total number (as shown in Figure 2-6). Those with whom you aren't friends will also

70

have a +1 icon and a corresponding link to Add Friend. Click a name to view a potential friend's Profile page (if available), to further identify them. Also, you may perform searches by category. You can also ignore any of those options and just browse or search by name.

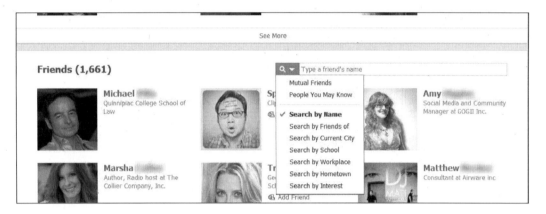

Figure 2-6

2. You can search through the list (looking for a specific person) in two ways: by typing the person's name in the Search box or by scrolling down the list and viewing each friend individually. When you find someone who isn't already your friend on Facebook, click the +1 Add Friend link to the right of that person's entry to send a Friend Request.

3. If you send a request by accident, or change your mind, click the Friend Request Sent button to reveal a drop-down menu where you can cancel your request, as shown in Figure 2-7. You will be asked to confirm your cancellation. Click Yes, and no one will be the wiser.

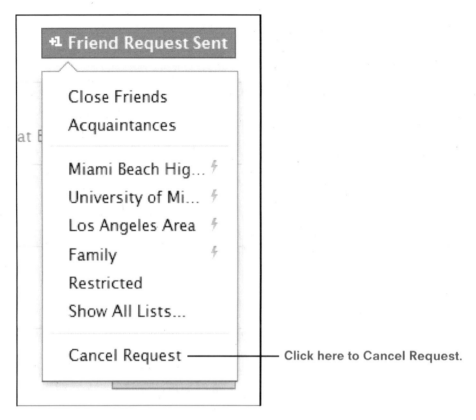

Figure 2-7

Accepting a Friend Request

When you become a Facebook member, someone may want to be your friend on Facebook. There are two ways you will be notified of a Friend Request. You get a notification via e-mail, and you find out when you log on to Facebook by looking at the Navigation bar. If you received your notification via e-mail, you can click the link contained in the message, and you'll go directly to the request. Since I'm not big on clicking links that arrive in e-mail, I log on to Facebook to view my Friend Requests.

1. Take a look at your blue toolbar on the top-left of your page: The button resembles the silhouette of two people. If you have a new Friend Request, you see a small red box with a number in it, overlapping the icon. To access your Friend Requests, click the icon.

2. When you click the icon, a drop-down menu listing your Friend Requests appears. At the bottom of the box, click the See All Friend Requests link so you can go to a full page to examine these requests more closely.

3. Once you have accessed your Friend Requests, you'll see your potential friend's photo and name. (This is why posting a good photo of you is important.) You will also see if you have any mutual friends with this person (and how many). By clicking the words *Mutual Friends* under the potential friend's name, you can see which friends you have in common.

4. To respond to a Friend Request, click one of the two buttons to the right of your potential friend's name.

One button reads *Confirm Friend* and one reads *Ignore*. Clicking those buttons will (respectively) add a friend or ignore the request quietly. If you ignore a Friend Request, you can still find it at the bottom of your All Friend Requests page.

When you ignore a Friend Request, no e-mail is sent to the person who placed the request. That person won't know that you chose to ignore him or her, except for the fact that you didn't accept the request. (Oops?)

The Navigation Bar Gets You Around

Whenever you visit Facebook, you see a blue bar at the top of the page. This Navigation bar, as shown in Figure 2-8, appears on all Facebook pages. The Navigation bar does just what its name implies: It allows you to navigate to different pages on Facebook quickly. From here, you can get a brief view of what's going on with your Facebook account. At top-left are small red squares with white numbers over icons. If you have no notifications for a category represented by an icon, no red box will appear over it.

Figure 2-8

1. Check out the activities available from the Navigation bar. In Figure 2-9, for example, I can see that I have 2 Friend Requests, 31 new messages, and 33 notifications. Clicking these icons will do different things:

   Keep in mind that anything you can do by clicking these icons you can also do from your Home page.

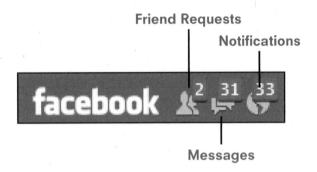

Figure 2-9

- **Friend Requests:** When you click this icon, you'll see a drop-down menu showing those who have requested your friendship online. You can click their names to go directly to their Profiles.

- **Messages:** You have this many messages from other Facebook members in your message area. You may view previews of their messages here, and click to go directly to each message.

- **Notifications:** If someone has posted a note on your Wall, commented on a post of yours, commented on a picture you're in, or made a comment in a Group you've joined, it's a notification. Click the Notification icon, and you'll get a drop-down listing like the one shown in Figure 2-10 with notifications clearly lined up and ready for a response.

Figure 2-10

2. Are you looking for something on Facebook? Not only your friends, but your local coffee shop (if it has a fan page, it may post coupons), your favorite movie, book, TV show, or author may have a page. Try out the Facebook search feature. Just start typing the Public person's name or topic in the Search box, and a drop-down list appears. As you type the words, Facebook uses a drop-down list to suggest a name (or topic) that matches what you are typing. If you see what you're looking for, click that name or phrase. If the name doesn't show up, click See More Results at the bottom of the drop-down list and search from there.

If you don't see a See More Results link at the bottom of the menu, odds are there's no match on Facebook. You can still try to search by clicking the little magnifying glass in the Search box and get more results.

3. Clicking the Home link at the right of the Navigation bar takes you to your Home page, the hub for your

News Feed and all your invitations and (most important) the organization area on the left side of the screen. This area gives you access to other Facebook activities, including adding photos and communicating with your friends. (Later Chapters 3 and 4 cover these activities.)

4. Clicking your name on the Navigation bar takes you to your Timeline page. From there, you can see what your friends have posted on your Wall as well as edit any information on the page.

5. Next is a down arrow that, when clicked, gives you links to the following areas.

   ■ **Account Settings:** You see this link unless you haven't signed up any Friends on Facebook — in that case, you'll see the words *Find Friends* before the Account Settings link. Once you've connected to a few friends, what you see here is only a link to your Account Settings.

   Click the Account Settings link and arrive at your account area, where you set your preferences to control how you operate on Facebook. (I cover the details in Chapter 5.)

   ■ **Privacy Settings:** Here's the hub I know you'll want to visit. This area is where you get to establish who or what (like a Group) gets to see your information on Facebook. You decide how private you want to be and make the relevant settings here. I offer more coverage of this information later in the book — also in Chapter 5.

Connecting to a Facebook Network

Facebook gives you the chance to become part of a network. *Networks* (in Facebook-speak) are groups of people who have similar hometowns, backgrounds, workplaces, or interests. This networking feature allows you to easily connect with your current or past coworkers or classmates, and helps you to be easily identified. To start the simple task of joining a network, choose Account Settings from the top navigation bar.

1. When you arrive at your My Account page, select the Networks line and click the Edit link that appears, as shown in Figure 2-11.

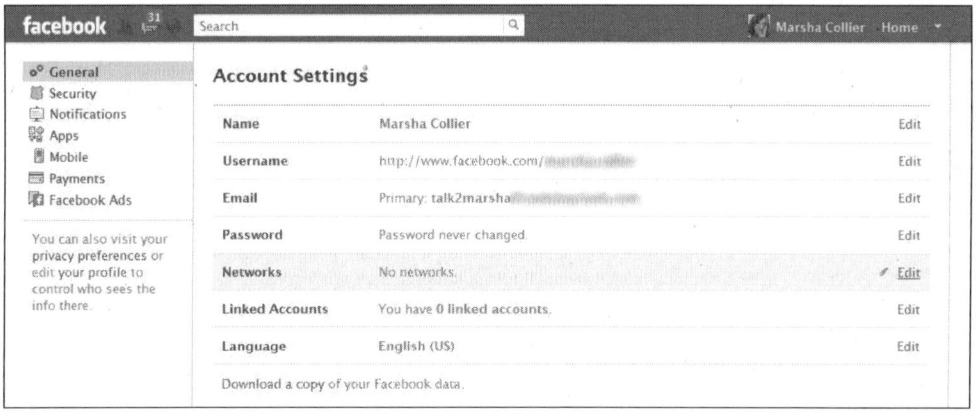

Figure 2-11

2. Clicking Edit will bring up the opportunity to join Networks. Click the Join Networks link.

3. Enter a city, workplace, school, or region in the Network name text box. The auto-fill feature shows you the names of networks that match what you're typing.

I typed *Los Angeles* because I live and worked there, and got the results shown in Figure 2-12. My former employer was the *Los Angeles Daily News,* so I would have to type in more letters to make the search more accurate.

When you select an employer network, you're often asked for your e-mail address so Facebook can confirm your employment.

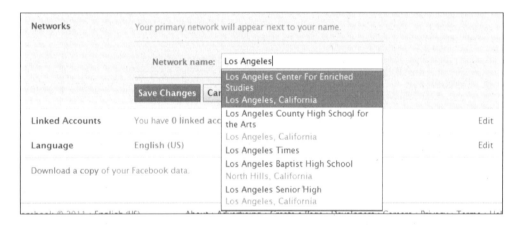

Figure 2-12

4. After you fill in any required information, click the Join Network button. Facebook sends your request, and all you have to do is await confirmation.

Chapter 3

Friendly Interactions

Now that you've delved further into building your online profile and have found a few friends, it's time to communicate. Facebook is all about connecting (do I sound like a broken record?), and your fun really starts when you start talking to your friends on the site.

tech 2 to connect

activities

- Updating Your Status
- Liking or Commenting on a Friend's Status
- Deleting Updates or Comments
- Removing Friends' Comments from Your Wall
- Removing a Tag from a Post
- Chatting in Real Time through Chat or Video
- Asking Your Friends a Question
- Sharing News and Information from the Web

In this chapter, you explore the fine art of posting, chatting, liking, and sharing. You'll learn how to add your news items into the Facebook Home stream for your friends to see — and how to (oops) delete items when you've made a mistake. See a news story you like on the Web? Share it! See one of your friends online and want to text (even video) back and forth? Go for it! Or learn how to turn your computer into stealth mode so no one will know you're online. Hurry and get started. . . .

Updating Your Status

In social media vernacular, the phrases *update your status, post to your page,* and *write a Wall post* all mean the same thing — that you type in a thought or phrase on your Facebook Profile page. This activity is where the fun really begins.

Look for the rectangular box that appears just below the cover photo and information at the top of your Timeline page (see Figure 3-1) or when you click the Update Status link on your Home page (see Figure 3-2).

Status update box

Figure 3-1

Figure 3-2

Then follow these steps:

1. Inside the Status Update box, you may see the question *What's on your mind?* The box may also be blank, but it's still where you get your point across. Just click inside the box and type any message you wish. Most people use this feature to let people know what they're doing at that given moment; often you see quick notes such as "Baking cookies for holiday gifts" or "Going to work out on the treadmill." I've also seen cryptic comments, general greetings, and pithy quotations; here you can say some of what "says it" for you.

   Status updates must be less than 63,206 characters, which should be enough for even the most detailed posts. When you're posting your update, you can also attach videos, photos, events, or links to interesting pages on the Web (more on that in the "Sharing News and Information from the Web" section later in this chapter).

2. If you'd like to include (or *tag*) one of your Facebook friends in your post, you can. Simply type the friend's

84

name as part of your status update, and a menu will appear showing matching names. In Figure 3-3, I'm about to mention my friend, Copper — notice how the drop-down menu appeared?

Figure 3-3

3. Click your friend's name to highlight it and make it appear in your update's text: Not only will he or she be mentioned on your update, but the update will also appear on his or her Facebook Timeline page! The name will also become a link! How's that for sharing?

   Sometimes the tagging feature lags or doesn't work. Try retyping your friend's name with an @ sign in front (as in *@Copper*); that will usually get Facebook working like a well-oiled machine again.

4. The best updates keep the message short and sweet. When you're done typing the message (and attaching a photo, video, or link), click the drop-down menu (as shown in Figure 3-4) to select whether you want to make the post private — or visible only to certain people or groups. To further privatize your posts, click the See All Lists link.

5. Click the Post button at the bottom-right of the Status Update section. Your page will refresh, and your comment will be live for the entire world (or whomever you've designated) to see!

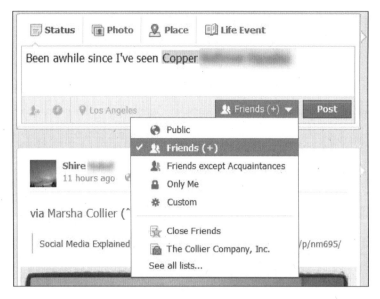

Figure 3-4

 The words you type in your status update appear beside your name at the top of your Facebook Timeline page. This communication is what keeps people tuned in to what you're up to, and makes them feel like they're plugged into your daily activities.

Liking or Commenting on a Friend's Status

The day will come when a friend says something in a status update that you really like or want to comment on. Facebook makes it easy to express yourself — just go ahead and comment in the box provided! If you can't think of something to say about your friend's posting, you can simply *Like* it, which is Facebook's version of giving a thumbs-up. Liking someone's post is a generous way to compliment without having to think about something pithy to say.

Figure 3-5 shows one of my friend's postings that I liked.

To Like a posting:

1. Click the word *Like* that appears at the end of your friend's post.

2. The word then changes from *Like* to *Unlike* (in case you change your mind, you can click Unlike and your approval will be withdrawn).

3. A comment box will open up after you click Like, encouraging you to communicate further. It's up to you whether to participate.

To comment on a posting:

1. Click the words *Write a comment* or merely start typing your comment into the long, thin box that reads *Write a comment* below your friend's post.

2. If you'd like to type more than one paragraph, do not hit your Enter key. Press the Shift and Enter keys on your keyboard at the same time to create a new paragraph or line break within a comment.

3. Once you've finished your tome, press your Enter key and the comment will appear under your friend's post.

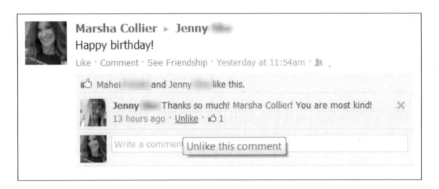

Figure 3-5

Deleting Updates or Comments

For one miniscule moment in the history of Facebook, members could edit status updates after clicking Post. This is no longer the case. If you post something and see a mistake later, you'll have to delete what you've posted and repost it — hopefully this time without repeating the error.

Here's how deleting works:

1. Find the status update or comment you left on your Timeline that you'd like to delete (you can do this at any time after the update is posted).

2. Hover your mouse pointer over the top-right corner of the post (as shown in Figure 3-6). When the Star and Pencil icons appear, click the Pencil icon: A drop-down menu appears from which you can delete the post.

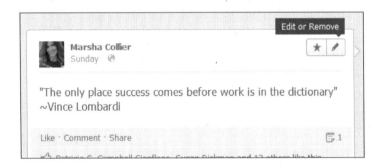

Figure 3-6

3. Choose Delete Post from the menu, and *poof!* — it's gone. If you *cross-posted* (tagged a friend in the post) to a friend's page, the post will disappear from that location at the same moment you delete it from your page.

89

Removing Friends' Comments from Your Wall

Occasionally an overzealous friend might post something to your Timeline page that makes you feel a bit queasy. Perhaps it's a political comment or something you don't want your kids to see on your page. Follow these steps to settle your stomach:

1. Hover your mouse pointer over the top-right corner of the post you want to remove and small Star and Pencil icons will appear in the corner, as shown in Figure 3-7.

Figure 3-7

2. Click the Pencil icon, and choose the Delete Post from the drop-down menu (see Figure 3-8). One click, and it's gone with the wind. Keep in mind: If you delete one of your own posts, any comments that were made on it disappear too.

3. If you click the Star icon, the post will expand in size from single column to a post that goes across both columns of your Timeline page.

Figure 3-8

Removing a Tag from a Post

As I show you in the earlier section "Updating Your Status," you can tag friends in a Facebook post. And when you get tagged, it's a good thing — most of the time. Other times, you might not want to be identified with the post. It's easy to remove yourself from that association — without breaking your connection to the friend who posted it — as follows:

1. Hover your mouse pointer over the top-right corner of the item you want to remove from the post.

2. Icons that look like a star and a pencil will appear. Click the Pencil icon to make your edit.

3. Once you've clicked the Pencil icon, the drop-down menu appears. Then you have several options, as shown in Figure 3-9:

   - **Hide from Timeline:** This will leave your name tagged on the post, but will remove it from your Timeline page.

   - **Remove Tag:** Choosing this option will remove your name associated with the post. It will also then disappear from your page.

   - **Report/Mark as Spam:** If the tag is to something offensive, you can click here to make Facebook aware of the egregious post. It will also report the person who posted it as a spammer to Facebook.

4. Choose an option from the drop-down menu. The tag and/or post (depending on your choice) is now gone into the ethers.

Figure 3-9

Chatting in Real Time through Chat or Video

With Facebook's chat feature, you can see if your friends are on Facebook at the same moment you are. If you see a friend and would like to say *Hi,* you can. Facebook chat is similar to sending text messages back and forth with a friend — only it's a lot easier to do online than with a smartphone. That's because you have a nice big keyboard to work with. If your computer has a webcam, you can even *video-chat* (see and talk to each other in a video window using your computer's camera, microphone, and speakers). Check out Chapter 9 for more coverage of video chatting.

Just try the following:

1. In the lower-right corner of your Facebook Timeline or Home page, you will see a Chat box with a green dot (indicating you have friends online) next to it. Figure 3-10 shows the Chat box at the lower-right corner of my Home page. The number indicates how many of your friends are currently online.

Figure 3-10

2. Click the Chat box and it expands to show you a list of your friends. If they are online and available to chat, a green dot will appear next to each name.

3. Select a friend to chat with by double-clicking his or her name; then a chat window will pop up. If you want to chat with your friend, just start typing. Your friend will get a notification with your message and can then type back.

If your friends are not online at that very moment you type a chat message to them, they will see your message in their chat window when they return.

4. If you have a webcam and would like to video-chat, click the small video-camera icon you see at the top of the Chat box, as I did in Figure 3-11. If this is your first Facebook video chat, you'll be asked to download and install a small file. (This file is perfectly safe and will not affect your privacy.) Once setup is complete, you can initiate a video call (powered by Skype).

Figure 3-11

5. Enjoy your chat, via text or video. Once you are finished, just put your mouse pointer over the Chat box and click the X in the upper-right corner. Doing so closes out the chat and the view to your world will be closed.

If you would rather not participate in any sort of chat (or not let your friends know you're online), you can disable the chat feature by clicking the small Gear icon in the upper-right corner of the Chat box. Choose Go Offline from the drop-down menu to toggle your online chat status, as pictured in Figure 3-12. If you go offline, you are now free to peruse Facebook in stealth mode.

Figure 3-12

Asking Your Friends a Question

You may not have a burning question that needs answering, but questions are a great way to stir up some conversation. Facebook allows you to poll your friends and find out their opinions on the question you post.

Because Facebook made a bunch of changes in its format while I was writing this book, I thought I'd poll my friends for their opinions; Figure 3-13 shows what that looked like.

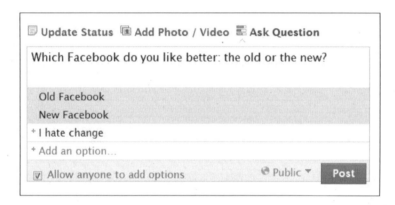

Figure 3-13

To post your own query for your friends, follow these steps:

1. Click the Home link at the upper-right of any Facebook page.

2. On the resulting page, at the top of your News Feed, you'll see three options:

   ■ Update Status

   ■ Add Photo/Video

■ Ask Question

Click Ask Question and a box will appear, as shown in Figure 3-13.

3. Type your question in the box. Then decide whether you want to offer your friends options to vote on.

4. If you want to offer options for your friends to select from, click Add an Option at the bottom of the text box and type in your options, line by line. (The options I added for my friends appear in Figure 3-13.)

5. If you want only a few people to see your poll, use the drop-down menu to select a group. If you don't mind who sees it, leave it at the default: Public.

6. When you're done, click Post, and your question will appear for all your friends to answer.

By the way, the results of my poll? It seems that no one likes the change very much!

Sharing News and Information from the Web

One of the best parts of being in the online world is getting the news from so many different sources. It's not just news stories, but also blogs, pictures, and even videos.

I address how to share videos in Chapter 4. For now, just start with baby steps and post a news story. When you've found a story on the Web that you'd like to share on your page, do the following:

1. Type your comment on the story in your Status Update box.

2. In a different browser tab, navigate to the website you want to share and select its URL by highlighting it in your browser's address bar. Then copy it by pressing Ctrl+C on your PC, or ⌘+C on your Apple keyboard.

3. Paste the URL to the bottom of your comment by clicking and pressing Ctrl+V on your PC or ⌘+V on your Apple keyboard. A mini-version of your linked page will appear in the box below.

4. Once the mini-version of your story appears, you can feel free to delete the URL from your comment post if you wish. The link stays with the mini-version, as shown in Figure 3-14.

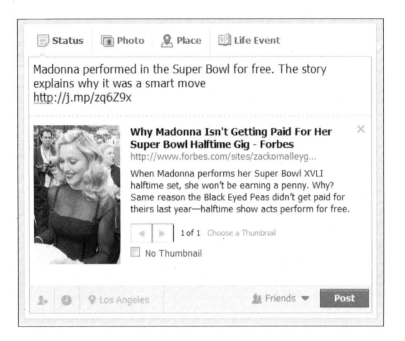

Figure 3-14

Chapter 4

Adding Photos and Videos to Your Timeline

Almost everyone's favorite part of Facebook is looking at friends' photos and videos on their pages. Since Facebook is all about sharing, it's up to you to share! Showing off photos of you, your family (that includes pets), and your friends is fun — and it gives your Facebook friends a chance to interact with you.

I know that you already uploaded an image to be your Profile photo, but what I talk about in this chapter is all the other ways to share photos and videos on Facebook.

So round up some photos and videos, and get started!

activities

- Copying Photos from Your Camera or Smartphone
- Storing Your Photos in the Cloud
- Uploading Your Photos to the Amazon Cloud Drive
- Downloading Your Photos from the Cloud Drive
- Placing a Photo or Video on Facebook
- Tagging Yourself or Your Friends in Photos
- Removing Tags and Photos from Your Timeline
- Deleting a Photo
- Creating and Editing a Photo Album
- Sharing a Video or Photo from a Friend's Page
- Sharing Videos You Find on YouTube

tech to connect

Copying Photos from Your Camera or Smartphone

I assume you're taking photos with a digital device — which can be your smartphone, an actual digital camera, or a separate device like a tablet. With these electronic wonders, you have more than one way to retrieve your images:

- **Cables:** Your phone, camera, or other device no doubt came with a cable that attaches to that device through a mini-USB port. The other end of the cable goes to a USB port on your computer (some devices also use this cable for charging).

- When you connect your device via this cable to your computer, you can explore the camera or phone on-screen, just as if it were a hard drive. You can drag and drop photos or copy them to your computer.

- **SD Card:** An *SD card* is a portable memory card that lives inside your camera to store your photos. High-capacity versions (SDHC cards) are commonly available, offering as much as 8 gigabytes (GB) of storage apiece; these cards can hold hundreds of photos.

  Most computers have a slot you can use to insert your SD memory card. When you do, you can read the tiny card just like a hard drive and treat it as such: Just copy or drag the photos from it to your computer.

- **Eye-Fi card:** The Eye-Fi card brings the magic of a Wi-Fi network direct to your camera. It looks, stores media, and fits into cameras just like a regular SD card (as you can see in Figure 4-1), but the Eye-Fi card has a built-in Wi-Fi capability that transfers photos and videos to your iPhone, iPad, Android device, or computer over a Wi-Fi network. You can also upload your photos to a personal Cloud space from Eye-Fi.

Figure 4-1

- **Cloud Upload:** Most smartphones (and some cameras equipped with the Eye-Fi card) can automatically upload your photos to Facebook, or a storage space on the Web.

- **E-mail from your smartphone:** Smartphones today are pretty doggone smart. They have the capability to e-mail photos directly from the phone.

Storing Your Photos in the Cloud

Would you like to store your files — not only photos, but important documents and music — in a place that's safe from the crashes and malware that can take your computer out of action? In the 21st century, many providers are offering Cloud storage. The *Cloud* is what these companies call a grid of computers with giant hard drives that hold the data you upload and download for storage on the Web.

Photos don't only come from your own computer, camera, or phone. What if you're visiting your children and you'd like to upload oodles of family photos from their computer? Uploading them to the Cloud is much safer than copying them to a flash drive that you might lose on the way home.

Many companies — including Snapfish, Photobucket, and Flikr — offer Cloud storage for your photos. These companies have varying policies regarding storage limits (some are unlimited) and varying costs (some offer free storage). I use Amazon.com as an example because I already have an Amazon account and it offers me 5GB of storage space for free. That's about 5,000MB of storage space, and as long as I have an Amazon account, I don't even have to buy anything (as of this writing). Amazon gives you the option to buy more storage space for a yearly fee based on the amount of space you need, and you can store any type of digital data, including music files.

Although each Cloud storage site has its own processes, you can use the steps in this section as a guide. Uploading your files to Amazon is pretty flawless.

1. Type www.amazon.com in your browser. You will arrive at the Amazon Home page.

2. Look on the left side of the Amazon Home page and find the navigation menu. Hover your mouse pointer over Amazon Cloud Drive and choose Your Cloud Drive from the fly-out menu (see Figure 4-2).

3. The resulting page will ask you to sign in.

   ■ If you are an Amazon customer, type in your e-mail address and password and click the button that says *Sign in using our secure server.*

   ■ If you are not an Amazon customer, type in your e-mail address and select the option button next to *No, I am a new customer.* Click the button that says *Sign in using our secure server* to proceed.

Figure 4-2

4. The next page (Figure 4-3) is the Amazon registration page with several items to fill in:

   ■ Type in your name and your e-mail address, which will already be filled in once. You are asked to type it again to guard against typing errors.

amazon.com   Your Account | Help

Registration
New to Amazon.com? Register Below.

My name is: _____

My e-mail address is: onlinecustserv@gmail.com

Type it again: _____

My mobile phone number is: _____ (Optional)

Learn more

Protect your information with a password
This will be your only Amazon.com password.

Enter a new password: _____

Type it again: _____

[Create account]

Figure 4-3

- Give Amazon your mobile number. This is optional, but should you make purchases from Amazon, you can sign up for delivery status updates via text messaging. (I've been a customer for over a decade and Amazon has never abused my mobile number.)

- Type in a password that you will use on Amazon and type it again in the box provided.

5. Click the Create Account button, and you'll arrive at your account Home page where you have access to your very own Cloud Drive.

6. Click the Your Cloud Drive link on the left, and you'll see the folder of your very own Cloud Drive, as shown in Figure 4-4.

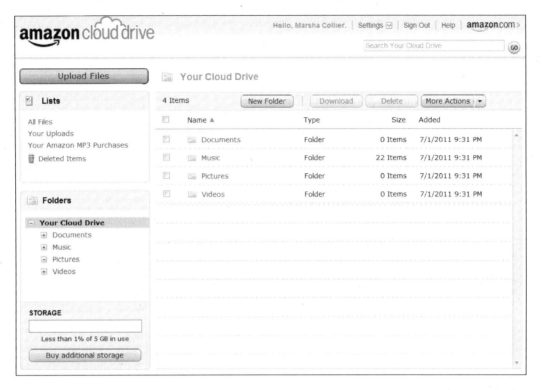

Figure 4-4

Uploading Your Photos to the Amazon Cloud Drive

Once you've uploaded your photos to your Cloud storage on Amazon, you can access them from any computer (or tablet) anywhere there is a Wi-Fi connection. To upload your photos to the Cloud Drive:

1. Click the Upload Files button under the Amazon logo at the top-left corner of the page.

2. Click the Your Cloud Drive button to select a destination folder for your files from the drop-down menu.

3. For your photo storage, choose Pictures from the menu and the Step 1 Your Cloud Drive button will change to say *Pictures* (see Figure 4-5), indicating that your photos will upload to the Pictures folder.

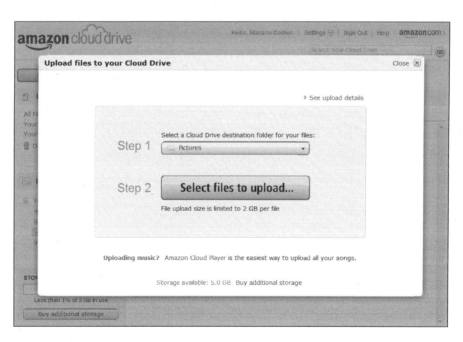

Figure 4-5

If you accidentally skip selecting a folder, your files will be uploaded into the Your Cloud Drive root folder. After your upload is complete, you can move or copy your files into a different folder.

4. Next, click the Select Files to Upload button; a folder on your hard drive will open. Navigate to the folder on your computer where your photos reside.

5. Select a photo by clicking it — or several files by clicking each file with your mouse while holding down the Ctrl key on your Windows PC (or the ⌘ key on your Apple keyboard).

6. When you've selected your photos, click Open in the lower-right corner to begin uploading your files.

7. Your selected images upload to the Your Cloud Drive storage for use anywhere, anytime.

Downloading Your Photos from the Cloud Drive

What goes up must come down, right? (At least eventually.) When you decide you'd like to download one (or a few) of the photos you've uploaded to the Amazon Cloud Drive — whether to another computer, a tablet, or a Wi-Fi–enabled device — the process is pretty cut and dried.

To download individual files directly from Your Cloud Drive, follow these steps:

1. From the left side of the Amazon Home page, find the navigation menu and hover your mouse pointer over Amazon Cloud Drive.

2. From the fly-out menu, choose Your Cloud Drive and Your Cloud Drive will open.

3. You will see four folders (as in Figure 4-6) in Your Cloud Drive:

   ■ **Documents:** For storing any documents you want to store in the Cloud.

   ■ **Music:** Any digital music you purchase from Amazon will appear here, as well as any MP3 file you choose to upload from your computer.

   ■ **Pictures:** Here's where you have stored photos from your computer.

   ■ **Videos:** Here's where you'd put any videos you want to upload.

4. Put your mouse pointer on the Pictures folder and click. Your folder with all the photos you have uploaded will appear.

Check mark files to download.

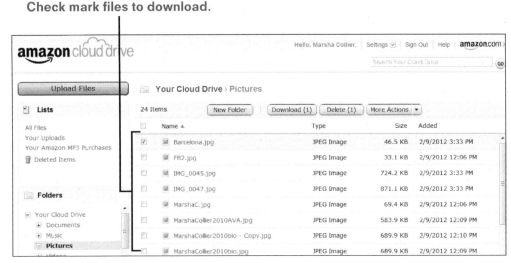

Figure 4-6

5. Check the box next to the file you want to download and click the Download button above your file list.

If you want to download several pictures, put check marks in the boxes next to each photo — they'll download one at a time to your selected location.

6. Your browser opens a dialog box where you can select where you'd like to download the selected picture.

7. When you've found the place you'd like your photos to reside, click the Save button in the lower corner of the window; the download from the Cloud will begin.

When you've found your way through all these options and have your pictures ready for the world to see, it's time for . . .

Placing a Photo or Video on Facebook

As with most Facebook activities, you have more than one way to post a photo or video. When you see something amusing you'd like to share, snap a picture! The easiest and best way to post a *single* photo or video is to post it directly to your Profile (Timeline) page.

1. Start by signing in to your Facebook account and navigating to your Profile page (click your name in the upper-right corner).

2. Type a message about the item you plan to post in the Wall posting box at the top of the left column that says *What's on your mind?*

3. Above your message, find the icon for uploading a photo (it looks like a little stack of photo prints, and the word *Photo* is next to it), as shown in Figure 4-7.

Figure 4-7

4. Clicking that icon changes the window to give you three choices. Here's how those choices work:

114

■ **Upload Photo/Video.** To upload a photo or video already on your computer, click the Upload Photo/ Video link. Your window changes to look like the one shown in Figure 4-8, with a Choose File button to select an item from your computer (or from an attached SD card or flash drive). Click Choose File and a dialog box opens; from here, you can look for a photo or video on your computer's hard drive. Find the one you want to upload and double-click it to select it. Your Status box now shows the name of the photo or video you selected, next to the Choose File button.

Figure 4-8

Before clicking Post to upload the photo or video to Facebook, you have some Privacy Settings to choose. Figure 4-9 shows the options that appear when you click the arrow next to the small globe at the bottom of the posting box. Click the appropriate Privacy option, and then click Post.

The photo or video uploads — and you see it in the Status Update.

115

Figure 4-9

■ **Use Webcam.** If you have a webcam on your computer and want to take a photo or film a video, click Use Webcam. If you're using a laptop computer, the webcam is most likely built in, with its lens facing you at the top of your screen. Clicking this option activates your camera automatically — and a warning appears (as shown in Figure 4-10). You must give the Adobe Flash Player permission to access your camera.

Figure 4-10

116

After you select the Allow option button and close the warning, your camera will have permission for this one time. You may notice that Facebook is prepared to film a video of you. Click the Switch to Photo button (see Figure 4-11) in the upper-right corner of the screen, and Facebook will switch your webcam to picture-taking mode. You'll see yourself in the camera — smile! After selecting your Privacy setting (I allow everyone to see), click Post.

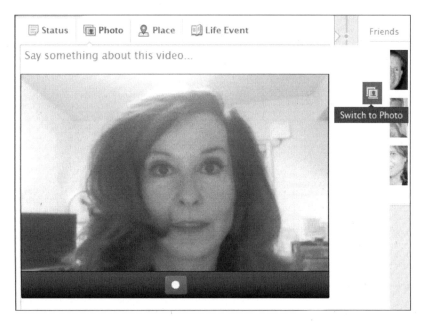

Figure 4-11

■ **Create Photo Album.** If you're ready to work with a batch of photos on Facebook, click Create Photo Album. I discuss this more complex task in the later section, "Creating and Editing a Photo Album."

Tagging Yourself or Your Friends in Photos

No matter where you find photos of you or one of your friends on Facebook, you'll be able to tag them (unless they have disabled this feature in their Privacy Settings). *Tagging* is the Facebook phrase for adding the names of friends to photo information. Tagging a friend makes the friend's name appear when someone hovers a mouse pointer over the tagged image. Tagging also links the photo to the appropriate profile. Whenever friends are tagged in a photo, that photo appears in their individual Timelines and becomes a permanent part of their Photos areas. (For more about Facebook Timelines, see Chapter 6.)

As long as your Privacy Setting is in effect, you receive an e-mail notifying you of your newfound fame every time you're tagged. By clicking the link in that e-mail, you can swiftly get online and look at the picture.

1. When you see a photo of you or one of your friends on Facebook, click it and you arrive at the photo's page. If no one has been tagged in the picture, no linkable names will appear when you mouse over the photo.

2. To the right of the photo you will see a Tag Photo link.

3. Trace your mouse pointer over the photo; a Like button and a Tag Photo button will appear at the bottom of the picture. You also find the name of the location on Facebook where the photo appears, as shown in Figure 4-12.

Figure 4-12

4. Click either of the Tag Photo links. Then move your cursor and click when it's on the nose of anyone in the photo. A box will come up, framing the face; so will a list of your friends, so you can select a name to put in the tag.

5. Start typing in your friend's name (or your name if the photo is of you), and Facebook narrows the selection as you type. I found my name in Figure 4-13.

Figure 4-13

6. When you've selected the name of the person in the photo, click his or her name: Bingo! The name of the person you tagged is now at the bottom of the photo — and the photo posts automatically to your tagged friend's Timeline page.

7. If you have more than one friend in the picture, repeat Steps 2 through 6 until you tag everyone. When you finish tagging friends in the picture, click the Done Tagging button below the picture.

You must be friends with someone on Facebook before you can tag that person. If you see a friend in a photo and you're not connected to him or her on Facebook, make a Friend Request. After the person accepts your request, you can tag your new Facebook friend.

120

8. As people view the photo, they'll see the tagged names at the bottom. If they move their mouse pointers over the picture, the person's name pops up.

Removing Tags and Photos from Your Timeline

You may get an e-mail and find that one of your friends has tagged you in a photo on Facebook. Excited, you log on to your Timeline page . . . and groan. Have no fear — if you find a photo that a friend has taken of you that doesn't quite meet your standards, you can do something about it. Follow these steps:

1. Find the photo on your Timeline. Move your mouse pointer over the photo (without clicking): A Star icon and a Pencil icon magically appear.

2. Move your cursor over the Pencil icon (as in Figure 4-14) and an Edit or Remove label appears.

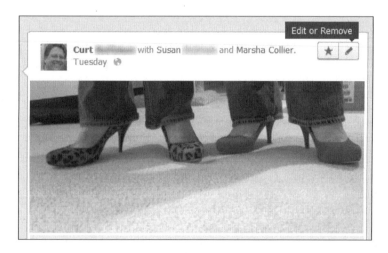

Figure 4-14

3. Click the Pencil icon and another dialog box appears, giving you several options:

- **Change Date.** Clicking here allows you to put in the correct date the photo was taken so it will find the right spot in your Timeline.

- **Add Location.** Add the location the photo was taken so it will show up as a mark on your Timeline Map. ***Note:*** Adding a location to a photo makes that information available to anybody viewing your Timeline. And so, think twice about whether adding a location might compromise your security.

- **Hide from Timeline.** Clicking here removes the photo from your Timeline. If you click it in error, don't fret. A button to undo your mistake appears immediately.

- **Remove Tag.** Here's what you're looking for (instructions continue in the next step).

- **Report/Mark as Spam.** If the photo is something totally unrelated to you — especially if it's anonymous and/or obnoxious — click here and the Facebook user who posted it will be reported for Spamming.

4. Clicking Remove Tag opens a window like the one shown in Figure 4-15. Here you need to give Facebook a reason for wanting to remove the tag — fortunately, just "wanting" to remove it is okay. Facebook asks for the reason to find out whether nefarious goings-on were in progress when the photo was posted or tagged — or whether the photo violates Facebook policies.

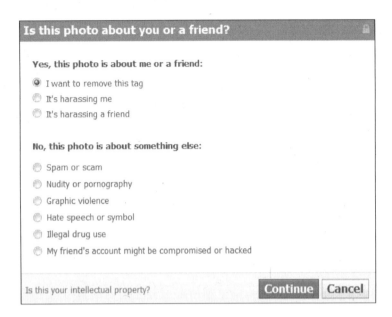

Is this photo about you or a friend?

Yes, this photo is about me or a friend:

- ⦿ I want to remove this tag
- ⦾ It's harassing me
- ⦾ It's harassing a friend

No, this photo is about something else:

- ⦾ Spam or scam
- ⦾ Nudity or pornography
- ⦾ Graphic violence
- ⦾ Hate speech or symbol
- ⦾ Illegal drug use
- ⦾ My friend's account might be compromised or hacked

Is this your intellectual property?   **Continue**   Cancel

Figure 4-15

5. Click your mouse to highlight the option button next to *I want to remove this tag.* (If there is a different reason, select it from the dialog box and click there.) After you indicate that you want to remove the tag, click the Continue button at the bottom.

6. A new window opens, giving you three option buttons to select from:

   ■ **Remove the tag *<friend's name>* created.** Clicking this option button removes the tag and will remove the photo from your Timeline. The photo will still be visible in other places unless your friend removes the photo from Facebook.

   ■ **Ask *<friend's name>* to take the photo down.** This option will send a message to your friend asking to take the photo down. Facebook suggests (as do I) that this is the best way to remove the photo from Facebook. Hopefully your friend will post better photos in the future.

- ■ **Block _\<friend's name\>_.** This is the Facebook equivalent of having your friend walk the plank: Click here and you will no longer be able to contact each other on Facebook. You may still be able to see the photo and the tag on other friends' profiles.

Should you ever decide to unblock someone you've previously blocked on Facebook, it's easy: Just manage your Blocked List on the Privacy Settings page.

7. Click Continue and the tag goes away into the Facebook ether, never to be associated with your name on Facebook again. It will remain in the friend's album, but someone would have to view the photo to see the image of you. After you've untagged yourself in a photo, _no one but you_ can tag you in that particular photo again.

8. To merely remove a photo from your Timeline and not banish it forever, select the Hide from Timeline option outlined in Step 3.

If you've accidentally tagged the wrong person in a photo, you can undo your error by clicking the Remove Tag link.

Deleting a Photo

1. If you upload a photo by mistake — or simply decide you'd rather not keep that photo-taken-with-your-ex online — you can remove it. You can delete only the photos that you, personally, have uploaded.

   If you want to disassociate yourself from a photo that someone else uploaded, you'll have to settle for untagging yourself (see the preceding activity in this chapter).

2. Move your mouse pointer over the photo (without clicking): A Star icon and a Pencil icon appear. Click the Pencil icon and an Edit or Remove dialog box appears. (This option only removes the photo from your Timeline, and does not delete it completely.)

3. Click the photo to get to the Photo page and find the small Cogwheel icon in the upper-right corner.

4. If you click the down arrow next to the small Cogwheel icon, a menu will appear and show you some options, as shown in Figure 4-16.

Figure 4-16

5. Choose Delete This Photo from the menu, and (poof) the photo is gone from your Facebook Page.

Creating and Editing a Photo Album

Facebook has many ways to get to the page where you can create photo albums, but some are easier than others. You can get there quickly from your Timeline page by clicking the Photo link in your Status Update box; then click the Create Photo Album link.

1. In the resulting dialog box, navigate your computer's folders to locate the photos you want to include in your photo album. Click to select a photo to upload, hold down the Shift key if you want to select more than one, and then click Open.

   As your photos upload, you see a progress bar that shows you that indeed, your photos are flying through the webbytubes up to Facebook.

2. You arrive at the Create Album page. There you type a title for your album in the box above the words *Say something about this album,* type a location in the Where Were These Taken box, and add a date by clicking the Add Date link. Adding the location of the place the photo was taken adds the photo to your Timeline Map.

3. Select your Privacy Settings for the album by clicking the Public (default) button in the lower-right corner and choosing from the resulting menu. I've got things all set up in Figure 4-17.

Figure 4-17

At this point, you can click the +Add More Photos button to open a folder on your computer to select other photos you want to upload. Once the page is completely loaded, you can type a caption beneath each photo.

4. To tag your friends in a photo, click their noses; a box will pop up. Start typing a name in the box, and a list appears with matching names; choose the right one. Be sure to click your own nose and tag yourself as well. The moment you tag a photo, it appears in the Timeline of the friend you tagged.

After you have tagged each photo, the names of the people you have tagged will appear at the bottom of the photo, as shown in Figure 4-18.

129

Figure 4-18

5. To place the photos appropriately in your Timeline, click the small Clock icon that appears below each picture; then, from the drop-down menus (shown in Figure 4-19), select the year and month. Add the day the picture was taken (if you want) and click Save.

Figure 4-19

6. Facebook likes to have a Cover photo for each album. Select the photo that you'd like to appear as your Cover, and then click in the upper-right of the photo. A menu drops down. Then, from the menu, you can choose to make that photo your Cover image — or even to delete the image if you decide you don't want it in your album (see Figure 4-20).

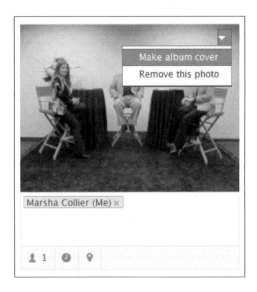

Figure 4-20

If the uploading process causes you a problem, try clicking the Try the Basic Uploader link. Doing so opens a dialog box (as in Figure 4-21) that prompts you to browse your computer, one photo at a time, and upload photos individually. When you're done uploading photos, you can then give each photo a location and date, and tag your friends.

Upload Photos to Untitled Album

Browse...

Browse...

Browse...

Browse...

Browse...

Upload Photos Cancel

Figure 4-21

To add photos to an existing album, go to your Timeline page and, below your Cover picture, click the Photos link. This brings you to a page with any existing photo albums you have and the most recent photos that you have uploaded (or photos that friends have tagged you in). Click the album you want to add to, and it opens (as I've done in Figure 4-22). In the upper-right corner is a link to Edit Album. Click the link and add photos or information pertaining to your album.

BlogWorld & New Media Expo 2011
By Marsha Collier (Albums) · Updated last Friday · Taken at Los Angeles Convention Center · ✎ Edit Album

Figure 4-22

Sharing a Video or Photo from a Friend's Page

Every now and then, you might see a photo or video posted on a friend's page that you'd like to share with your other friends. Facebook makes it easy to do so with the Share option.

1. On the post with the photo or video you're interested in, find the Share link and click it.

2. A window opens where you can add a comment (just as you do on your own Wall posts), so type a few words, as I did in Figure 4-23.

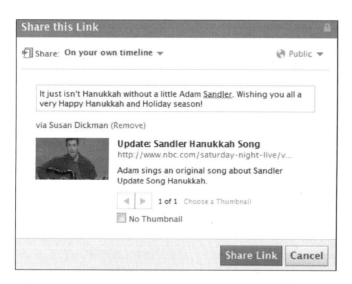

Figure 4-23

3. Click the down arrow for the Share drop-down menu at the top of the Share This Link dialog box. The resulting menu gives you options to share the image or video

on a friend's page or within a private message, as well as to post on your own page.

4. You can also select Privacy options (for who can see the shared post) by clicking the Public button in the Share This Link dialog box.

5. When you've filled in all the little details and you're ready to go, click the Share Link button and the image or video will appear on your own Timeline (or wherever you've directed it). As shown in Figure 4-24, I shared a photo 21 minutes ago, and it has already been Liked seven times and Shared by someone else once.

Liked seven times.

Shared once.

Figure 4-24

Sharing Videos You Find on YouTube

People burn many more hours watching videos on YouTube (www.youtube.com) than you or I can possibly imagine. YouTube bills itself as the "Broadcast Yourself" site, so you'd think that you might find only homemade videos. But that's not the case. You also see big-time studios posting portions of television shows and trailers for films.

While there are other sites where you may want to download videos, none is as popular as YouTube. YouTube has become an Internet phenomenon and has reshaped the way entertainment is consumed. A few statistics? YouTube hosts 2 billion video views a day and receives 48 hours of uploaded video every minute. The result is nearly 8 years of content uploaded every day! Users upload the equivalent of 240,000 full-length films every week, and more video is uploaded to YouTube in one month than the three major U.S. networks created in 60 years! You can visit the site at www.youtube.com.

Follow these steps to find and share a YouTube video:

1. To find a video to share, start by typing a keyword in the Search box on the Home page at www.youtube.com. You can search for topics, actors, singers, politicians . . . just about anything.

    For example, I typed *Susan Boyle* (of *Britain's Got Talent* fame) in the search box and got over 83,000 hits. And one of my favorite films is *One Six Right,* an independent film on the history of aviation. To find it, I type *One Six Right* into the text box and click Search. Try typing a search term for one of your favorites.

2. On the next page (the search results), you see a list of videos that match your search term, as shown in Figure 4-25.

3. To share a video that you find on YouTube, click the Share button that appears below the video viewing window. A box opens below the viewing window, showing you the URL of the video and a collection of buttons that link to various online communities — including Facebook. In Figure 4-26, notice that the Google+, Twitter, and Facebook icons appear alongside Email and Embed buttons.

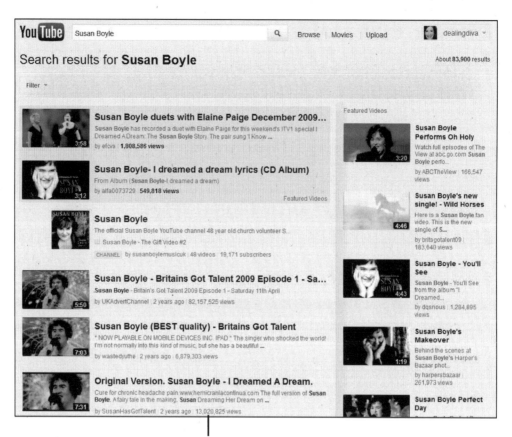

Millions of views.

Figure 4-25

Figure 4-26

4. To share the video on Facebook, click the Facebook button. A window appears and offers you a few ways to Share, visible from the Share drop-down menu that you access by clicking the down arrow. The drop-down menu gives you these options for posting: On Your Own Timeline, On a Friend's Timeline, In a Group, or In a Private Message.

■ To post the video to your own Facebook Timeline, type your message in the Write Something text box (see Figure 4-27) and click the Share Link button. The window closes, and the video and message are posted to your Facebook Timeline page.

■ If you'd prefer, you can post the video on a friend's Timeline (or in a private message) to a Facebook

139

friend. Click the On a Friend's Timeline from the drop-down menu. You then see a Facebook message window, as shown in Figure 4-28. Begin to type your Facebook friend's name, and a list will appear. Select your friend's name from this list, and the message is ready to send. Click the Share Link button to post the message or send it along to your friend's Facebook Message Center.

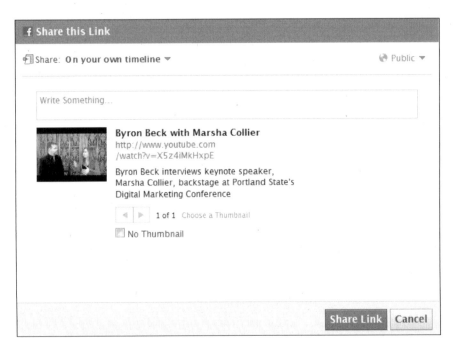

Figure 4-27

5. If you're already on your Facebook Page when you find a video, you can copy the link that showed up in the link box when you clicked the Share button under the YouTube viewing window. After you copy it, paste it directly under the comment you type in your Status Update box. Figure 4-29 shows you how the video will load automatically onto the page before you click Post.

140

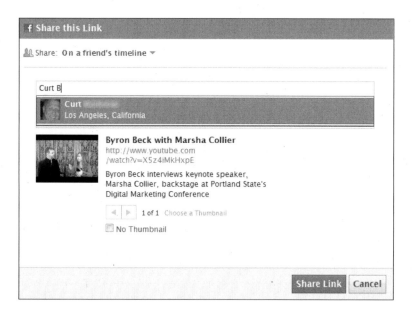

f Share this Link

👥 Share: On a friend's timeline ▾

Curt B|

> **Curt** ▓▓▓▓▓▓▓
> Los Angeles, California

Byron Beck with Marsha Collier
http://www.youtube.com
/watch?v=X5z4iMkHxpE

Byron Beck interviews keynote speaker,
Marsha Collier, backstage at Portland State's
Digital Marketing Conference

◄ ► 1 of 1 Choose a Thumbnail

☐ No Thumbnail

Share Link | Cancel

Figure 4-28

Please wait while your video is uploading.

Cancel

50.39 MB of 58.63 MB (115.7 KB/sec) -- 1 minute remaining

Enter the following info while you wait for your upload to finish.

In this video: 2011 Los Angeles Holiday Train
Tag people who appear in this video.

Title: Los Angeles Metrolink Holiday Train in its 15th Year

Description: ventura, Orange County, Los Angeles and San Diego counties) brings a brightly packaged gift – a 450-ton train decorated with holiday displays, a musical performance and 50,000 twinkling lights – and of course, Santa!. You can check the schedule here: http://www.metrolinktrains.com/news/?id=7144

Privacy: 🌐 Public ▾

Save Info

Figure 4-29

If you don't like the way the URL looks when you type your post — no problem. Just wait until the video loads in the posting box and then delete your copied URL. The video will still post. If you change your mind and decide not to post the video, just click the small *x* in the upper-right of the video box. The video will be deleted from your Facebook Page forever (or till you change your mind).

Popularity on YouTube

So what are most people watching on YouTube? As of the end of 2011, the video that's had the all-time most views — **675,428,876** — is *Baby ft. Ludacris* from Justin Bieber. But, as if to prove that popularity doesn't just belong to the big guys, the sixth most popular (with over **397,136,684** views) is *Charlie Bit My Finger — Again*. It's a short home movie about an infant biting his older brother's finger, as shown in this sidebar picture. Go figure. I guess there's a big audience for kid videos; after all, the *Little Rascals* episodes are getting harder to find these days (unless you look for a boxed set of DVDs on eBay).

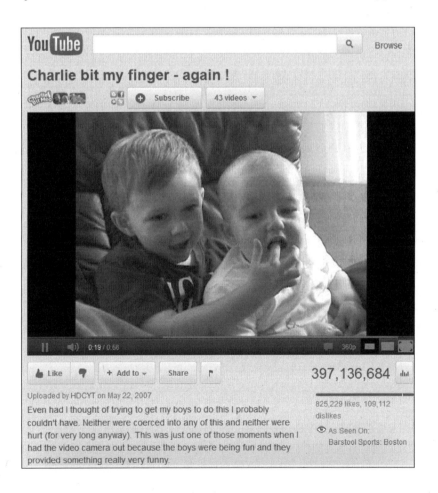

Chapter 5

Fine-Tuning: Account and Privacy Settings

As you may have read in Chapter 3, tuning the Privacy level of your individual Wall posts is something you can do as you go along. When you look deeper into the core of Facebook, you find many other places where you can make tweaks — as often as you want — to enhance and safeguard your online experience. Facebook is also always

activities

tech 2 to connect

- Customizing Account Settings
- Making General Settings
- Selecting Security Settings
- Setting Your Notifications
- Managing Apps, Mobile Access, and Payments
- Making Item-by-Item Privacy Settings

making changes, so I recommend that you revisit the Account and Privacy Settings areas of the site at least every couple of months or so. In this chapter, I give you the 411 on what settings to look out for and which ones to set up initially on your account.

Customizing Account Settings

You may think that Privacy Settings are crucial — and they are — but Account Settings are the most important. If you don't set up your Account correctly, you might not enjoy the time you spend on Facebook as much as you would with the right settings. You have several areas to fine-tune on the Account Settings. So, you might want to get started.

1. Sign in to your Facebook account and find the down arrow on the far-right end of your blue navigation bar.

2. Click the arrow and a drop-down menu, as shown in Figure 5-1, appears.

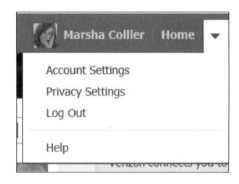

Figure 5-1

3. Choose Account Settings from the menu, and you will be brought to the Account Settings page.

When you reach the Account Settings page, the settings from the first area — the General area — are showing on the right. But you also see these other areas in a list on the left: Security, Notifications, Apps, Mobile, Payments, and Facebook Ads. You can access any area by clicking its name on the left. The following sections tell you about your options for each set of settings.

 Remember you can also edit settings directly on your Timeline to control who sees your posts and photos.

Making General Settings

The General Account Settings area represents the basics that identify your Facebook account. Nothing fancy to worry about here; Figure 5-2 gives you a look at this area, which you can use to access your basic information. To fine-tune any of the information stored here, you start by clicking the Edit link next to the item you want to change.

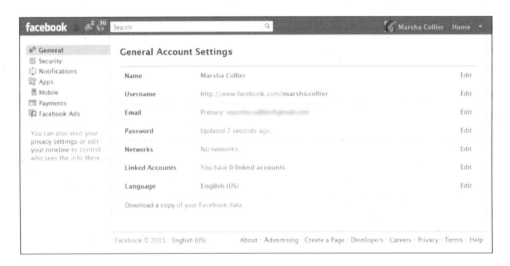

Figure 5-2

Here's what you find under General Account Settings:

- **Name:** The name you used when you registered on Facebook.

- **Username:** Becomes the URL for your Facebook Profile page. If you click Edit, you can get a personalized URL for your Profile page (just like a vanity license plate). Type your desired username and find out whether it's available. If not, try variations such as marsha.collier, mcollier, marshac — you get the idea.

- **Email:** Your registered e-mail address appears here. If you click edit, you'll see (as time goes on) other e-mail addresses that you use will appear here. This amazes and disturbs me. Although I may have used another e-mail when I signed on to Facebook, for some reason Facebook now lists five of my e-mail addresses! This situation is just another lesson that anything and everything you put on the Web is fair game.

- **Password:** Here you will see the last time you changed your password. For your security, I recommend that you change your password at least every couple of months. To do so, follow these steps:

  1. Click the Edit link.

  2. In the text box provided, type your old password for security.

  3. In the next box, type your new password.

  4. Type your new password (again) in the third box — to be sure you spelled it right — as shown in Figure 5-3.

  5. Click Save Changes.

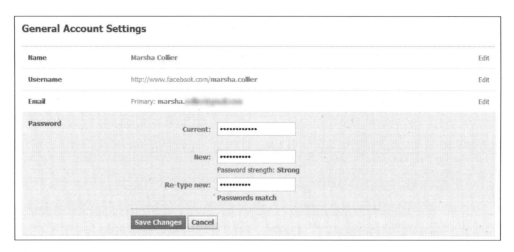

General Account Settings

Name	Marsha Collier	Edit
Username	http://www.facebook.com/marsha.collier	Edit
Email	Primary: marsha. ███████	Edit
Password		

Current: ••••••••••••

New: ••••••••••
Password strength: **Strong**

Re-type new: ••••••••••
Passwords match

Save Changes   Cancel

Figure 5-3

When you change your password, Facebook will send a notification e-mail to all e-mail accounts they have registered for you. This is for your protection.

■ **Networks:** If you join networks of people, such as alumni from an old school or coworkers from your employer, they will appear here. (I know — I'm just not a joiner.) You can join a network by following these steps:

1. Click the Edit link.

2. The window opens a shaded area that tells you *Your primary network will appear next to your name.* Under that, click the Join a Network link.

3. Start typing the appropriate network name in the text box, and Facebook's drop-down menu will suggest existing groups based on what you type, as shown in Figure 5-4.

4. When you see your intended network on the menu,

click it and its name will appear in the text box.

5. Add more networks by clicking the Join Another Network link and following the same procedure as above.

6. When you've added all your networks, click Save Changes.

Figure 5-4

You can join networks at any time you wish and leave them just as easily.

■ **Linked Accounts.** If you have chosen to link other sites — for example, Google, Yahoo!, VerisignPIP, OpenID (and more) — they show up here. When you log in to those linked sites, you will be logged in automatically to Facebook. My browser holds my passwords, so I do not link accounts.

Using an Internet password generator

If you're at a loss about how to select an uber-secure password, see my suggestions in Chapter 1, or you can find help on the Web. A software company, PC Tools, has a free password-generating tool at www.pctools.com/guides/password/. Using this widget enables you to make the strongest password possible — which is a good thing! The bad part about a strong, secure password is that it may be very difficult to remember.

The figure shows how I've generated an industrial-strength password, including numbers and mixed-case letters. If you like to write down your passwords on a list, I recommend that you copy and paste the supplied phonetic pronunciation. Somehow, *YANKEE - alpha - FOXTROT - ROMEO - uniform - SIERRA - tango - Eight - delta - romeo - Nine - sierra* is easier for me to make sense of than *YaFRuSt8dr9s*.

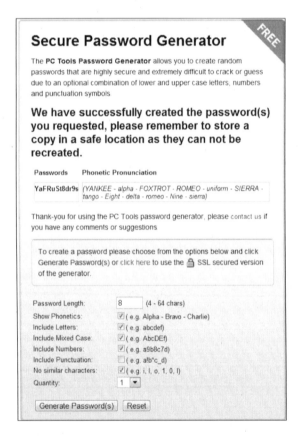

- **Language.** If you're not in the mood for your native tongue, you can click Edit and select from dozens of foreign languages. Just for fun, you might (briefly) try English (Pirate) or English (Upside Down) — it's always good for a laugh.

- **Download Your Facebook Data.** In a link at the bottom, you can click to download all data from Facebook. This is a worthwhile place to visit once your Facebook Page has been active for a while. The download will include

  - Your Timeline information

  - Timeline status updates, comments, photos, and content that you and your friends have posted to your Timeline Wall

  - Photos and videos that you have uploaded to your account

  - Your Friend List

  - Any notes you have created

  - Events to which you have RSVP'd

  - Your sent and received messages

You have good reasons for downloading Facebook data. If you've lost your phone that contained photos that you uploaded only to Facebook, you can retrieve them. You might want records to archive for the future — and it's just one other way to control what you share (by having a copy of it).

Selecting Security Settings

It seems to me that Security and Privacy might be one and the same but they are not. Security is more about your safety online, while Privacy helps you regulate how much you want to share, and with whom. Here are some of the settings (pictured in Figure 5-5) that you might want to check out:

Security Settings

General	
Security	
Notifications	**Secure Browsing** — Secure browsing is currently **enabled**.
Apps	**Login Notifications** — Email notifications are **enabled**.
Mobile	**Login Approvals** — Approval is **not required** when logging in from an unrecognized device.
Payments	**App Passwords** — You haven't created App Passwords.
Facebook Ads	**Recognized Devices** — You have **21** recognized devices.
You can also visit your privacy settings or edit your timeline to control who sees the info there.	**Active Sessions** — Logged in from **Northridge, CA, US** and 8 other locations.
	Deactivate your account.

Figure 5-5

■ **Secure Browsing.** This is a most important security setting. Click the Edit link to place a check mark (if there isn't one) in the check box that says Browse Facebook on a Secure Connection (https) When Possible. This keeps your online surfing on a secure channel.

■ **Login Notifications.** So what if someone figured out your password and logged in from his or her computer? Wouldn't you like to know? Putting a check in the box next to Email will cause Facebook to send you an e-mail anytime your account is accessed from a device (computer, tablet, smartphone) that you've never used before. (You might be signing in from your kid's iPad, right?)

- **Login Approvals.** If you'd like to be hyper-vigilant about access to your Facebook account, you can require that a security code be entered any time a new device tries to access your account. Signing in from a new device will cause Facebook to send a code via SMS (text messaging) to your phone. You will then have to type in the code you just received before you can access your account. If this seems like a good idea to you, click Edit, put a check mark in the box, and you'll be walked through the process.

- **App Passwords.** App passwords are one-time password access codes. Some Facebook apps can't receive security codes. If you're using an app that doesn't — and you have Login Approvals (which require such passwords) set up — you may be temporarily locked out of the app. So if you use (say) Skype through Facebook, you can generate an individual password to securely sign in to your apps from that platform. For more on how to use Skype and other Facebook apps that may interest you, see Chapter 9.

- **Recognized Devices.** When you have Login Notifications set up (as I do), you are asked to type the name of the device you're using to log in. Once you register a device, you will no longer receive e-mails when you log in again from that device. This entry shows a list of the devices that you have used to log in to Facebook.

- **Active Sessions.** This setting shows you the location from which you are currently logged in.

■ **Deactivate your account.** Clicking this link will cause your account to vanish! Your Timeline and all information associated with it disappear from the Facebook site immediately. From that point on, people on Facebook will no longer find you in search or view any of your information. If you feel you've been hasty and choose to return to Facebook, you can reactivate your account by logging in with your e-mail address and password. Your Timeline will be restored in its entirety (friends, photos, interests, and so on).

 Facebook's capability to restore your account after it has been deactivated should give you an idea about how permanent things can be on the Internet. This permanence is another good reason to think twice about what you post — before you post it!

Setting Your Notifications

Setting your notifications sounds benign enough, but it is one of the most important settings on Facebook. You see, once you have a bunch of friends, they will interact with you in any of dozens of ways on Facebook. Facebook will send you an e-mail every time an event happens.

If someone clicks Like on a post of yours — you get an e-mail. If a friend posts a comment on his or her own Timeline — you get an e-mail. Basically, anytime one of your friends hits a key to touch Facebook, you will get an e-mail. This can be more annoying than beneficial.

When you select Notifications on the left side of your page, you will initially see a listing of all interactions your friends have had with your page in the past few days. Most importantly, as in Figure 5-6, there is a box you can click to tell Facebook to send you a digest of these notifications as a summary — versus one as each event happens. This gets more important when you become active in many Facebook Groups where there could be hundreds of posts a day.

Notifications Settings

We send notifications whenever actions are taken on Facebook that involve you. You can change which applications and features can send you notifications.

Notifications are being sent to **marsha.**   (email).

Email Frequency:
☑ Send me important updates and summary emails instead of individual notification emails [?]

Recent Notifications

Sent Today

Clinton   sent you a request in MyCalendar - Birthdays.

Clinton   sent you a request in My Calendar.

Fabrizio   likes your photo.

Bob , David , and 3 other friends like your link.

Jeff   sent you a request in Millionaire City.

See More (9)

Figure 5-6

If you'd like to go through every possible notification and decide whether to give them individual permissions, you may, but it may take a very long time. Requesting the digest will solve this issue quickly.

Managing Apps, Mobile Access, and Payments

Pretty much, this area is for the most advanced Facebook users, but no doubt, you'll be one soon. So here's a quick rundown of what you can find in these three areas of settings.

■ **Apps:** In this area, you can see all the apps that you give permission to access your account during your time on Facebook. You give permission when you participate in a game or post from certain websites. On this page, you can view all the apps and decide whether you want to relinquish permission by removing them. Figure 5-7 shows you some of the things you can do.

Remove an app or its permissions.

App Settings

You have authorized these apps to interact with your Facebook account:

K Klout	Less than 24 hours ago	Edit ×
M Mashable	Last logged in: Less than 24 hours ago	Remove app
This app can:	**Access my basic information** Includes name, profile picture, gender, networks, user ID, l...See More	Required
	Access my profile information About Me and Birthday	Required
	Send me email Mashable may email me directly at marsha.collier@gmail.com	Required
	Post to Facebook as me Mashable may post status messages, notes, photos, and videos on my behalf	Remove
	Access my data any time Mashable may access my data when I'm not using the application	Remove

Figure 5-7

It's not a bad idea to check this list, even for apps you regularly use because their settings may have changed since you signed up. You can see which connections to your account that they require to function and which may be removed.

If you'd like to remove some of the optional app permissions, just click Remove and they will be gone!

■ **Mobile:** As you'll find out right away, Facebook loves to send you stuff in your e-mail. If you're feeling a bit lonely and would like to be pinged by Facebook on your cellphone with SMS messages, here's where you can give them your number.

■ **Payments:** Playing games on Facebook is generally free. Some games allow you to purchase "virtual" goods. If that sounds silly to you, give a listen: Let's say you play a game that requires you to have a car. Your car needs gas to run, right? The game may give you the opportunity to win some fuel, but your tank may need to be topped off. That's where the virtual goods come in. You can buy what you may need, in this case, gasoline for your virtual car.

Facing Facebook Ads

You can control how you interact with ads on Facebook to get the benefit of seeing what your friends "like" while keeping your personal information private. Click the Facebook Ads tab (refer to Figure 5-2) to adjust your settings. You'll see a description and two sections that you can edit: Ads Shown by Third Parties, and Ads and Friends.

1. At the time of this writing, Facebook does not *officially* give third parties the right to use your name or picture in ads. In the Ads Shown by Third Parties section, click Edit Third Party Ad Settings, and you'll go to a new page.

2. The drop-down menu on this page gives you two options that manage your information should Facebook's current third-party policy change. Your picture and name may be shared on Social Plugins (click the link provided in the Ads Shown by Third Parties section to read more). To prevent Facebook from becoming over-generous with your likes and dislikes, or, in the future, allowing a third party to use your name or picture in their ads, choose No One from the drop-down menu.

3. Click the Save Changes button to exit.

4. In the Ads and Friends section, click the Edit Social Ads Setting link.

5. To share the least information, choose No One from the Pair My Social Actions with Ads For drop-down menu. If you choose the other option on this menu,

you share information about your social actions (what you've Liked and Shared) with Only My Friends.

6. Click the Save Changes button, and you're all set!

The Ads and Friends area also gives permission for advertisers to use your Facebook "likes" and preferences to tie in with their ads. If you're curious about what a social ad might look like, see Figure 5-8.

Denver Sushi

The best sushi in Denver. Try our daily lunch specials for $9.95. Fan our page for special offers.

👍 Like· Marsha Collier likes this.

Figure 5-8

Tightening Up Your Privacy Settings

Privacy is what everyone hears about in the news, but as the preceding section shows, staying safe online is not just about privacy. Your online safety takes many forms. Keep in mind that you can always manage the Privacy Settings of your status updates, photos, and Profile information by using the inline audience selector (see Figure 5-9) as you post on Facebook.

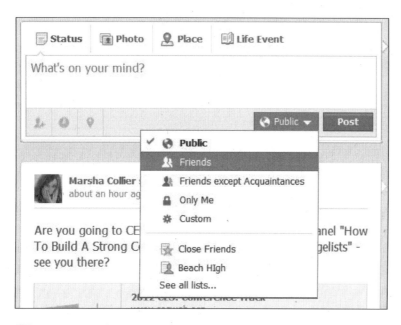

Figure 5-9

You will see several options for defining your privacy that are repeated throughout this section. It's helpful to have definitions for these options as you decide which setting to choose:

■ **Public:** This broad option means anyone, everyone,

and search engines like Google, Bing, or Yahoo!.

- **Friends:** This option includes the people who've accepted your request for friendship on Facebook — as well as people whose requests for friendship you've accepted.

- **Friends of Friends:** This option comes with the assumption that your friends' friends are vetted — since they are friends of your friends. Choose this option when you trust that your friends make good connections.

- **Friends Except Acquaintances:** When you accept people as friends on Facebook, you have the option to indicate that they are Acquaintances with the understanding that you may leave them out of some of your posts and other actions online.

- **Specific People or Lists:** This option enables you to identify more specifically those who can see your posts.

- **Only Me:** This option doesn't show up too often. I figure if I want Only Me to see something, why post it on Facebook to begin with? (This option is one of the choices when you register and input your birthdate.) You can also choose this option to restrict who can post on your Timeline to just you.

When you determine Facebook Privacy Settings, you have two types to consider: privacy when you post and the default setting. Follow these steps to take care of the default Privacy setting:

1. From any Facebook page, click the arrow next to your name on the top-right and choose Privacy Settings

from the drop-down menu. Here you set the default for any posts. This setting is in control of privacy for all your posts — unless you change it for an individual post or update. This setting is especially useful for some smartphone apps that don't have a privacy option that covers posting.

2. Select the option button next to one of the three choices, as shown in Figure 5-10. In this case, I selected Public because I don't post anything that is too personal or that I don't want others to see on my Timeline. If what I want to say is private, I send my friend a message through his or her Profile page and make it a Private Message. Learn how to send private messages in Chapter 8.

Figure 5-10

3. If you want to customize your privacy by using one of the options described at the beginning of this section, select the Custom option button. In the resulting Custom Privacy dialog box, choose from the various options in the drop-down list, as shown in Figure 5-11. These choices limit viewing to your circles of Friends, Friends of Friends, Specific People or Lists, and so on.

Figure 5-11

4. Viewing can also be more selective. You can choose to allow viewing by the Friends of people who are tagged in a post or photo. Select the Friends of Those Tagged check box to put a check mark there.

5. You may also exclude any one person or group in particular by typing the relevant name in the text box in the Hide This From section of the dialog box.

6. Click the Save Changes button when finished with Custom Privacy.

Making Item-by-Item Privacy Settings

For each of the individual additional settings below the default privacy selections (Public, Friends, and Custom), you start by clicking the link to the right of the setting you want to manage (see Figure 5-12). For example, follow these steps for the How You Connect section:

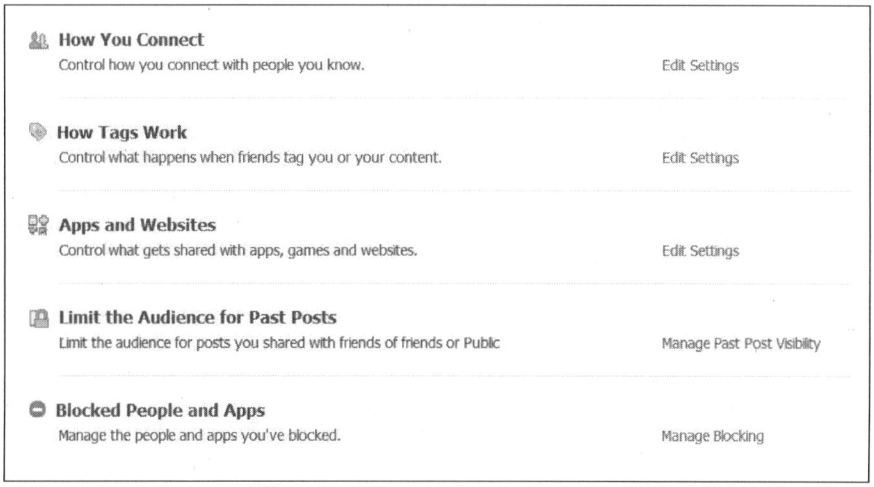

How You Connect
Control how you connect with people you know.   Edit Settings

How Tags Work
Control what happens when friends tag you or your content.   Edit Settings

Apps and Websites
Control what gets shared with apps, games and websites.   Edit Settings

Limit the Audience for Past Posts
Limit the audience for posts you shared with friends of friends or Public   Manage Past Post Visibility

Blocked People and Apps
Manage the people and apps you've blocked.   Manage Blocking

Figure 5-12

1. From the main Privacy Settings page, click the Edit Settings link next to How You Connect.

2. You'll see the How You Connect dialog box with options similar to those shown in Figure 5-13. Click the down arrow for the lists on the right side to make changes for each item.

3. When you're finished making your selections, click the Done button and return to the main Privacy Settings page.

Figure 5-13

The other individual Privacy Settings include the following:

■ **How Tags Work:** People can tag you on Facebook — either in photos or posts. If you want to control tagging, this area will come in handy. You can decide whether you would like to approve any tagging activity that appears on your Facebook Timeline. By clicking the Edit Settings link, you get the items and options as shown in Figure 5-14.

Timeline Review of posts friends tag you in before they go on your timeline (note: tags may still appear elsewhere on Facebook)	Off >
Tag Review of tags that friends want to add to your posts	Off >
Maximum Timeline Visibility of posts you're tagged in once they're on your timeline	🌐 Public ▾
Tag Suggestions when friends upload photos that look like you	Off >
Friends Can Check You Into Places using the mobile Places app	On >

Figure 5-14

- **Apps and Websites:** Here's where you can withhold your information from the third-party partners of Facebook. By clicking Edit Settings, you can decide what is shared and what is not.

  The only approval I give on this page is for my Profile to be listed on search engines through Public Search. It's the best way for old friends to find you when they don't look on Facebook first.

- **Limit the Audience for Past Posts:** When people have used Facebook for a long time, they might not want to go back and edit the Privacy Settings of all the posts they've made over the years. Use this option as a one-click solution to making old posts private.

- **Blocked People and Apps:** If there is someone on the planet whom you never want to find you on Facebook, you can block him or her from access to your account here. Once you block someone, that person cannot (or can no longer) be your friend on Facebook — or interact with you at all on Facebook (except within apps and games you both use and groups to which you both belong).

169

You can also add friends to a Restricted list where they can see only the information and posts that you make Public. Facebook does not notify your friends when you add them to your Restricted list.

Chapter 6

Facebook Timeline — Your Virtual Scrapbook

Remember back in the day when you'd be invited to someone's house and you'd sit (or perhaps sleep) through a slide show outlining every detail of the latest European vacation? The pictures were no doubt lovely, but you were at the mercy of the person controlling the speed and narrating the show.

activities

tech 2 to connect

- Making Your Timeline a Reflection of You
- Placing Your Cover Image
- Adding Life Events
- Changing Your Profile Picture
- Adding to Your Map

Or how about when you visit relatives and they take out the old photo albums? Do they hand them to you? Probably not. Your friends and family want to guide you, step by step, through pages and pages of photos.

These two instances might be more significant experiences if you were able to peruse the images at your leisure, asking your own questions; on your own time. That's what a well-thought-out Facebook Timeline can do for you and all your friends. So, in this chapter, I show you how to make such a Timeline.

Making Your Timeline a Reflection of You

Your Facebook Timeline is an illustrated chronicle of your travels and activities — and much more. Timeline can be a life history, or a family history of sorts, if crafted properly. It can show how you categorize your life and times and digitally document your entire life, should you wish. If my mom had a Facebook Timeline that I could have downloaded — with all her notes and photographs — what a treasure it would be. And quite a legacy!

There are several segments to your Facebook Timeline (which I tell you more about in later sections of this chapter):

■ **Cover Image.** Use this photograph almost like a billboard. It appears above your Profile picture. In the next section, I give you some ideas about what sort of photo to put in this space. Figure 6-1 shows you the kind of cover image that would make me smile if that lovely young lady were related to me!

Below the right side of the cover image on your own Timeline, you'll see three items in a row: Update Info, Activity Log, and a clickable Cogwheel icon.

173

Figure 6-1

■ **Profile Picture.** Your Profile picture (which you in-
serted when you signed up) is pictured at the bottom-
left of your cover photo. As you change the images over
time, Facebook archives the past ones in a photo album
named *Profile Pictures*.

For those just starting on Facebook

The Timeline feature was introduced on Facebook at the end
of 2011. It made things a bit problematic for those who already
were sharing hundreds of photos with their friends. They had to
go back and add locations and dates for the photos. I'm quite
sure that many felt it too onerous a task to do. Here's where
you have the advantage, if you're brand new to Facebook.
Starting fresh, you can build your Timeline carefully — sharing
only what you wish to share with friends, friends-of-friends, old
school chums, and even the public.

174

■ **Life Events.** When you have life events — graduations, new jobs, engagements, marriages, or almost anything — you can date the events and they become part of your online story. Because you didn't have the opportunity to share life events this way before joining Facebook, you can add them retroactively. Figure 6-2 shows a Life Event from my Timeline.

Figure 6-2

■ **Map.** Every photo or Life Event that you post can be *geo-tagged* when uploaded from a smartphone or tablet. Geo-tagging marks the items with the location in which they occurred, as shown in Figure 6-3. If you post photos and events from your computer, Facebook lets you tag the city, state, or country. But consider security, too. Do you want potential thieves to know that you're in Borneo and your house is empty?

- **Likes.** This box lets your Facebook friends know which business, fan, or Group Pages you've given the "thumbs up" to.

- **Photos.** Your Timeline links to every photo you have posted or has been tagged with your name on Facebook.

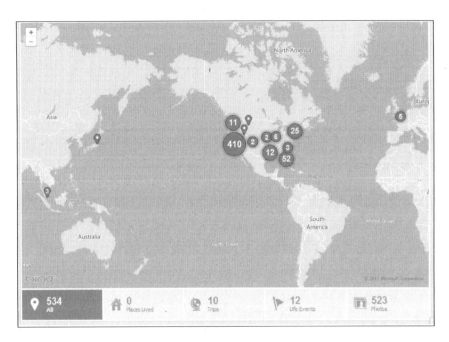

Figure 6-3

- **Subscribers/Subscriptions.** If you find some interesting folks on Facebook whom you'd rather not (or don't know well enough to) *friend* — that is, make into Facebook friends — you can still subscribe to their Timelines. The Subscriptions box lists the people you subscribe to; the Subscribers box lists the folks who have subscribed to your posts.

A realistic word about privacy . . .

There is much hue, cry, and handwringing about a lack of privacy on the Internet — perhaps reasonably. But how can you really expect anything you post online to be kept private when you're not paying for a service? If you want reliable privacy for your photos or information, simply don't post them anywhere on the Internet other than on a secure private Cloud you pay for. Everything online is searched, scanned, and archived somewhere, and the storage systems used are not always fail-proof. Even the National Archives and the Library of Congress currently catalog tweets from Twitter and tons of data that's available online. This information is considered part of our country's history.

David Ferriero, the Archivist of the United States of America, said, "Access to records in this century means digital access. For many people, if it is not online, it doesn't exist. The use of social media to increase access is the new norm. NARA [National Archives and Records Administration] has been going after innovative tools and projects that increase digital access to our records, including projects that invite public participation. We are developing a Citizen Archivist Dashboard that will encourage the public to pitch in via social media tools on a number of our projects."

That said, keep your correspondence private; do not post truly personal information online. Ever.

Placing Your Cover Image

Your Cover photo is the first thing that people see when they come to your Facebook Page. Your Profile photo appears in the lower-left side, inset into the cover. The Cover image is public, by default, as is your Profile picture. You don't have to add a Cover image — but why not? It can make your Page much more interesting.

You can use a personal photo, a photo you've taken out in the world somewhere — pretty much any photo that expresses your mood at the time. Figure 6-4 shows a happy family from Karen's Page. It's fun thinking of new cover photos to display. Facebook CEO Mark Zuckerberg uses a photo of his dog and remarks, "Timeline is the story of your life . . . a new way to express who you are."

Figure 6-4

Sometimes you just can't conjure up a photo to insert in your cover — for that I recommend visiting some of the sites below for some artistic ideas.

■ **CoverPhotoFinder** (http://coverphotofinder.com/): This site was started by two former Facebook interns. You can find hundreds of entertaining and interesting photos — featuring nature, architecture, animals, and more — you can upload automatically to your Cover Image. It allows you to sign in to Facebook and test out the cover photos before you upload them to your Facebook Page, as I did in Figure 6-5. Note that when you select a photo, it will have the title and "by (the photographer's name)." You can remove this text easily after uploading, just before clicking Change Cover.

Figure 6-5

- **FaceCoverz** (http://facecoverz.com/en): If you consider yourself a geek or have unusual tastes, you may find some interesting photos to upload automatically here. FaceCoverz (see Figure 6-6) lists hundreds of photos by topic, from "30 Seconds to Mars" to "Zonda." Photos are categorized there, and a Search box can help you find a topical photo that interests you.

- **coverphotoz** (http://www.coverphotoz.com/): Here's another site that not only has a large group of images, but has a cool tool (see Figure 6-7) you can use to cus-

180

tomize your images with added text, photo effects, and background color.

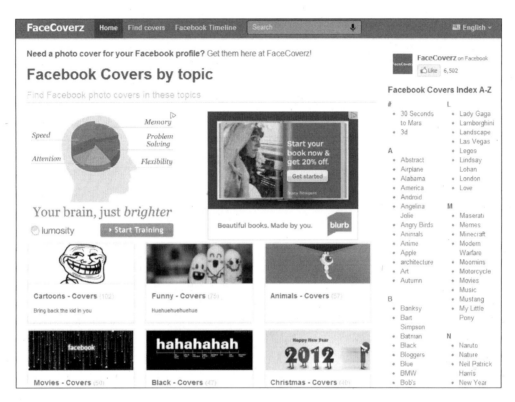

Figure 6-6

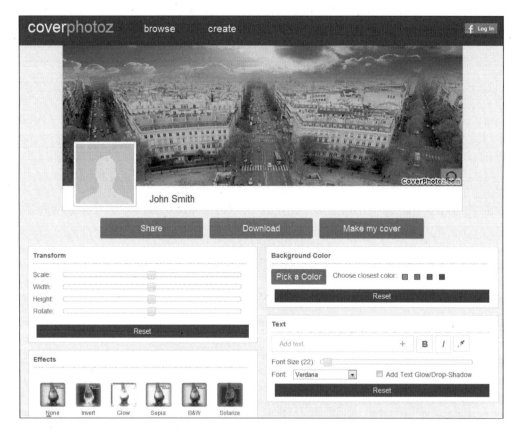

Figure 6-7

To insert a Cover photo in your Timeline:

1. Click the Add a Cover button to the left of the vertical Timeline bar on the right side of your Page. A dropdown menu will ask you to select a photo in one of two ways:

- **Choose from photos.** Clicking here opens the page of photos that you have previously uploaded to Facebook. Click the desired photo, and it will appear in your Cover Photo area.

- **Upload photos.** Selecting this option opens a window on your computer. Go to the folder that holds

182

your pictures, select one, click Upload, and the photo appears on your page.

The photo appears as 851 pixels wide by 315 deep. But I wouldn't be too concerned about the exact size; just stick to horizontal format pictures. Facebook will enlarge your photo to fit the space, and if it's too small, it will appear *pixelated* — that is, the photo appears chunky; the pixels are enlarged and therefore visible. Your photo has to be at least 720 pixels wide, or Facebook will ask you to select a different one. Try to stick with high-resolution photos when you can.

2. If your image is larger than 315 pixels in height, you have the option to reposition your image so that a distinct area of it can be featured horizontally. Over your image, you'll see the words *Drag to Reposition Cover,* as shown in Figure 6-8. You'll find when you mouse over the image, the cursor turns into a hand icon.

Figure 6-8

3. Drag the image up or down until you feel it's centered just the way you want it.

4. Click the Save Changes button and your image will appear at the top of your Facebook Timeline Page.

 When you want to change your Cover photo (or reposition it), mouse over the Cover photo. A Change Cover button will appear. Clicking it brings up the drop-down menu pictured in Figure 6-9; from there, make your selection.

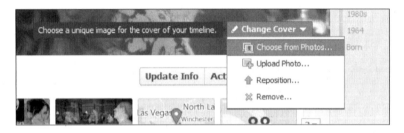

Figure 6-9

 As you make progress filling out your Timeline, you can always view it as others do: Just click the small Cogwheel icon under the right side of your Cover photo and select View As.

184

Adding Life Events

Life events happen to us all. And in Facebook's status box, you have the opportunity to share your special events with the world (or just with your friends).

1. To add a significant event, click the Life Event link above the Status Update box.

2. Select one of the five main categories that identifies your event. Facebook will produce a slider menu on the right (as shown in Figure 6-10) offering an exhaustive list of options in the main categories.

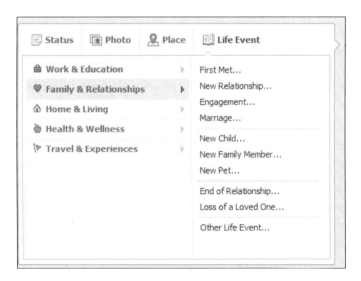

Figure 6-10

3. Select the category you wish to add and fill out the form that pops up, including the city and state in which the event occurred.

4. Add a photo. (Again, you can upload a fresh one or select from photos already uploaded.)

5. Specify the Privacy Setting by clicking the small down arrow to the left of the Save button.

6. When you're all done, click Save and the event will be part of your Timeline and on your map.

 Just clicking a year (or decade) in the Timeline navigation at the right of your Page will take you to that point in your Timeline.

Changing Your Profile Picture

If you've uploaded a Profile photo when you signed up, you may get in the mood to change it. I do recommend changing it every once in a while so your friends can get a new view of you. Give it a try.

1. Mouse over your Profile picture and a drop-down menu, like the one in Figure 6-11, appears. You now have several options:

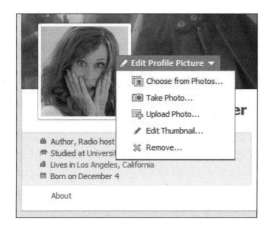

Figure 6-11

- ■ **Choose from Photos.** This will take you to your previously uploaded photos from your Facebook Page.

- ■ **Take Photo.** Got a webcam? Sit straight and smile pretty. Let your camera take a photo of you that will upload automatically.

- ■ **Upload Photo.** Select a photo from your computer to replace your current Profile picture.

- **Edit Thumbnail.** This allows you to reposition your photo to better center the image to your taste.

- **Remove.** Remove your Profile photo immediately (that's no fun at all).

2. To send Facebook a photo from your computer, click Upload Photo. A window from your computer will appear. Navigate to the folder in which your photos reside.

3. When you've found the photo, double-click the image in your computer or select it and click the Open button. After a little whirring on Facebook's part, your new Profile picture will appear in the Profile Picture box.

4. To adjust the way your new Profile photo is centered, mouse over the photo and click Edit Thumbnail from the menu.

Adding to Your Map

You'll notice a map below your cover photo on your Timeline. Click it, and you'll see a geographic map. You populate the map with special places whenever you add a Life Event or a photo that you tag with a location. You can also add to your map directly from the map.

1. Click the Map box below your Cover photo.

2. You can add photos to your map (if you didn't indicate location when you posted the image originally) by clicking the Add Photos to Map button. When you do, you see a filmstrip of the photos in your albums that have no locations specified. Facebook will ask, *Where was this?*

3. Type the location (city, state, and country, if appropriate) in the box provided.

4. Facebook produces a drop-down list of various locations that match what you're typing. The map will change to that of any location you select, as shown in Figure 6-12.

5. The photos will advance on the filmstrip until you have added locations to them all — or just until you get bored.

Figure 6-12

6. To save your locations and exit the map, click Done Adding.

Chapter 7

More Conversations via Pages and Groups

Y ou thought that the Timeline was fun? Wait till you hear about the many other ways you can use Facebook to your advantage to communicate with friends and family. You can build your own online communities — either publicly or privately!

Most of us have defined groups that affect our daily lives. There might be sports teams for the kids, religious or spiritual groups, volunteer groups, study groups, immediate family — you get the idea. Any group of people in your life can be defined in Facebook, and you can set up different ways to communicate with them. Although you can define Privacy Settings for your Timeline — deciding who gets to see your posts — you still see all your communications in that one spot. You can further enhance this online experience with Groups and Pages. In this chapter, I show you the difference between Groups and Pages, as well as how to interact with both.

Recognizing Pages and Groups

So what's the difference between the two? Pages and Groups, that is?

People and businesses use Pages as a public profile to keep their business (or public) life separate from their personal meanderings. People who tend to use Pages include musicians, sports stars, actors and actresses, writers, and politicians. On the business side, you find Pages used by brands, marketers, realtors, and magazines, to name a few.

Pages are not as versatile and don't have quite as much fun going for them as a personal page. For example, they don't have a Timeline, they can't send Friend Requests, and they can't interact with other Pages. But Pages often fills the bill for getting a presence online — especially if you're in a garage band! Following are some characteristics that distinguish Pages:

- **Privacy:** Page information and Wall posts are public and open to anyone who visits the page.

- **Members:** Anyone on Facebook is free to Like a page. Many brands have links on their websites that allow you to join their Pages with just one click, but I recommend that you don't rush right out and associate yourself with just anyone (or any business) until you've taken a look at the Page. Always check out the actual Page before you Like it!

- **Conversations:** Only the administrator of the Page can share posts under the Page's name. The Page's posts will show up in the Home page News Feed of everyone who clicked to Like the Page. Pages can also have customized navigation and apps. The administrator can also get statistics on the demographics of the members and use of the Page activity.

Joining a Group on Facebook can be a barrel of fun. I ~~wasted~~ spent many an hour conversing back and forth with my friends in a Group. It's great to find Groups that your friends have joined — or even find new Groups full of people who share interests similar to yours.

Groups can work as a substitute for mass e-mails you might otherwise send out to your family, friends, or any group you're a member of in the real world. If you'd like, you can set up your membership in a Group so that you get an automatic e-mail anytime a member posts a comment or status update. Here are some characteristics of Groups on Facebook:

- **Privacy.** Facebook allows much more privacy to members of Groups. Many Groups on Facebook are *Closed,* meaning that posts within the Group are visible only to members. Most other Groups (and their members) are listed in Facebook search; these are called *Open* Groups — anyone on Facebook can see the Group and the posts of the members.

There is an option for extreme privacy, the *Secret Group.* A Secret Group won't appear in search, and the only way people can join is if the administrator (or one of the members — if this option is set up) invites them. No one else will even know that a Secret Group exists.

■ **Members.** Initially the administrator invites and approves members. Other members of the group can invite others, but all must be approved by the admin.

■ **Conversations.** Members receive notifications in their notification center as new posts are placed in the Group. Members can opt in for e-mail notifications as well. Within a Group, you can post updates and photos to the Wall, ask questions, share documents, and schedule Group Events.

Finding Facebook Pages to Enjoy

Finding new Pages enhances your time on Facebook. It gives you the opportunity to learn new things about businesses, participate in contests, and meet others who are also fans. Once you find a Page you like, all you have to do is click the Like link to have full access. Keep in mind that if you change your mind, it's just as easy to click the Unlike link and remove yourself from the Page.

Contacting businesses and brands on Facebook can get many of your product questions answered, as well as help with customer service issues!

Do you use a favorite product? Read a certain newspaper like the *New York Times*? Use the product as an example, follow the steps, and see whether you can find the product's page.

When you perform a search on Facebook, the results will tell you whether and how many of your friends are already members of the Page or Group.

1. From any page on Facebook, type **New York Times** in the Search box at the top of the page.

2. As you type, a drop-down menu appears with the matches that Facebook finds for your text, as shown in Figure 7-1.

3. You may notice that your results may be sorted into several categories:

- **Groups.** If you're looking for a brand, fans of the brand may have started their own Pages to discuss things about the brand.

- **Pages.** These are either fan or business Pages or entries pulled from the Wikipedia.

- **Places.** When you tag locations in your photos, the locations will be in places. Many places have Pages (see the one for New York in Figure 7-2), where links to other Pages on Facebook reside.

- **Apps.** More on apps later, but apps are used to interact, play games, or do business with brands.

- **People.** If other Facebook members have brand Pages that match your search text, there will be a link in the list to their business Page.

- **Shared Links.** If links have been posted on Facebook that reference your search, they'll be listed.

- **More Results.** This option takes you to an All Results page that lists web-page results.

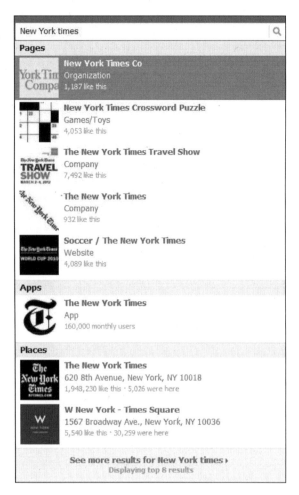

Figure 7-1

Figure 7-2

4. Click the Page that seems right and check it out. When I got to what I thought was the *New York Times* Page, I saw that it wasn't a Page from the "official" newspaper at all, but one put together by readers. (That's not what I was looking for.)

5. Return to the Search box and look through other Pages until you find the one that fits your needs.

You may come to a brand's Page that is *gated,* which means you can't really read what's going on until you click the Like button. Sometimes businesses do this to offer a sweepstakes or some other promotion. If you'd prefer not to Like a Page publicly until you know what's going on, go to the left side of the Page and click the Wall or Info link. Then you can investigate further before making your decision.

If you're receiving too many updates from a Page you've Liked, you can click Unsubscribe directly on the Page.

A few words about Pages . . .

Pages provide features that are not available in Groups. Both Pages and Groups enjoy the same type of interaction on their Walls, but Pages have more options you can customize and personalize. Facebook applications can only be used on Pages, so if you have a home-based business, you might just want a Page.

Keep in mind that Pages are open to the public and may only be created and managed by official representatives. If you would like to create a presence for a celebrity or organization and you're not officially authorized to do so, create a Facebook Group instead.

Creating Your Own Brand or Community Page

Lots of folks have hobbies that they like to share and what's more fun than sharing with others? You may have an interest that puts you out in the public in some way.

For example, actor Kevin Bacon and his brother have an indie band, The Bacon Brothers (with a Facebook Page); Kevin Costner, an entertainer in more ways than one, tours with his band, The Modern West (also with a Page on Facebook); one of my editors is also in a band (see the Page for The Common). A throng of interesting people who have Facebook Pages can be found at the Page called Discover Facebook Pages (shown in Figure 7-3).

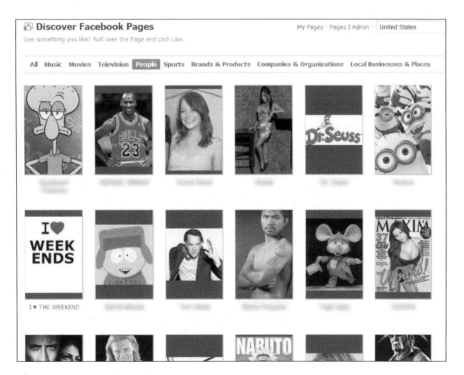

Figure 7-3

If you've got a passion for a topic and want to start a Page dedicated to it, or you're in the public eye and want to begin a Page as an "official" alternative to your personal Page, here's how you go about it:

1. You have two ways to get to the Facebook area where you can create your Page.

   - Go directly to the Discover Facebook Pages Page at www.facebook.com/pages.

   - If you don't feel like typing the URL, just go to the Facebook Page for any business or public figure, scroll down the column at the left side of the Page, and find and click the Create a Page link.

2. You'll arrive at the Create a Page (um) page. There you see a group of icons representing top-level categories; you'll have to decide which category you fall into and click it.

3. After you choose a top-level category, you see a drop-down list of more specific subcategories (see Figure 7-4). Choose one and further identify yourself by filling in the information requested by the subcategory.

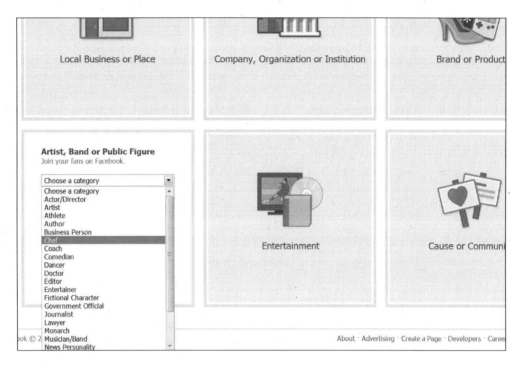

Figure 7-4

The six top-level categories to select from are

- **Local Business or Place:** Have a brick-and-mortar place of business? You'll need to select a subcategory and type in your address.

- **Company, Organization or Institution:** Just choose a subcategory and type in the name. Do you do taxes for people? Perform small business services? This might just be the spot for your Page.

- **Brand or Product:** This is where the big guys like Tide (soap), Samsung (electronics), Starbucks (coffee), and others build communities that you can join and participate in.

203

- **Artist, Band or Public Figure:** If you're uncertain as to what kind of public figure you are, there's always the *Fictional Character* category.

- **Entertainment:** Professional sports teams, TV stations, and more make their homes here.

- **Cause or Community:** If you have a cause or nonprofit, this may be the place for your Page. You may also have an area of interest where you can start a Community page (but keep in mind, anyone on Facebook can join a Page).

Once you've decided on the category and subcategory, putting together a Page is very much the same as setting up your own Page. You can also name other people to be administrators of your Page.

Here's how you get people to *Like* (or join) your Page:

1. Go to your Page and find the Invite Friends link in the administrator's column at the right.

2. A window where you can suggest your Page to your friends opens. If you want to invite just one or two friends, type the names of those particular friends.

3. The window also shows pictures of friends with whom you've had your most recent interactions. If the friend you have in mind to invite appears here, just put a check mark in the small box next to his or her picture. **Note:** Pictures of friends who already Like your page will be grayed out.

4. To search further, click the drop-down menu next to Recent Interactions. Cities you've visited, Groups,

schools, work (that you've told Facebook about), and a list of your personal categories show up, as depicted in Figure 7-5. Click any category here to see lists of those friends to invite.

5. You may also click the Search All Friends link and type each friend's name individually.

6. When you've selected all the friends you want to invite (and put a check mark in the small box next to each one's picture), click Submit. Facebook will send your friends invitations to your Page.

Figure 7-5

Discovering New Groups to Join

Finding a Group on Facebook is a similar process to finding a Page:

1. Think of a topic you're interested in and type that keyword into the Search box at the top of any Facebook page. Figure 7-6 shows you the top eight results of my search on *knitting*. The results are divided so that Open Groups show up plainly.

Figure 7-6

2. To find more Groups, Pages, and people who are into your topic, click the See More Results For link at the bottom of the results list. The next page will show you all results on Facebook, unfiltered.

3. To further refine your results — to see just Pages or Groups about your area of interest — click the Groups link in the left column of the Home page, as I did in my search shown in Figure 7-7.

When searching for interests on Facebook, you may get better results by refining your search to include only Pages, because many Groups may be Closed, or accessible by invitation only.

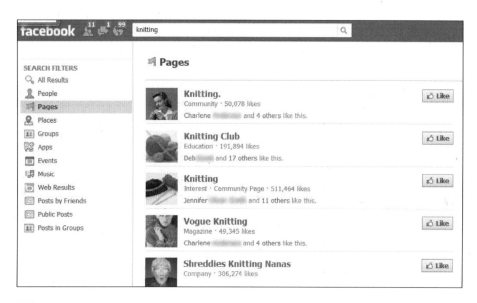

Figure 7-7

4. Click the title of any open group to see the Wall and check out what the group members discuss. If you click on a Closed Group, you won't see their Wall, but merely a list of members.

5. Once you've found a Group that strikes your fancy, click the Ask to Join button next to the Group's listing in the results (see Figure 7-8), or the button at the top of the Group's page.

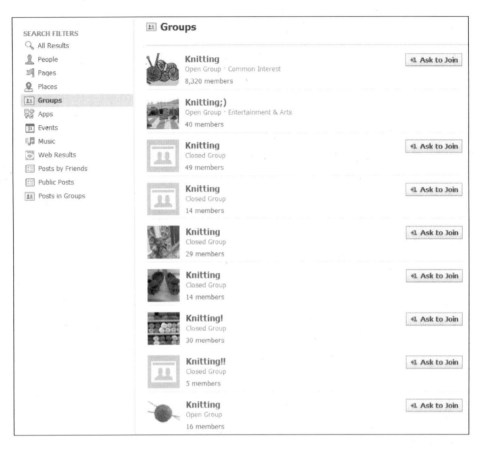

Figure 7-8

208

Starting Your Own Group

If you're interested in a particular topic, you may also want to create a Facebook Group. This way, you can discuss the topic with a whole new batch of other Facebook users and friends. From your Group, you can start a real-time chat, or send e-mail messages to everyone in the Group.

It's also a great idea to start a Secret Group with close family — perhaps another for close friends? That way, your conversations and private stuff will remain only among your closest contacts.

I just joined a Secret Group consisting of past employees of a newspaper where I worked. It's so much fun to be able to see what people were thinking behind the scenes 20 years ago. We bring up old memories; expose old gossip — a flash from the past! We're even thinking about planning a reunion. Do you have a group of people you knew in the past that may be on Facebook?

Members of your Group must be your friends on Facebook, so get family members to join!

To start a Group:

1. Go to your Home page and look for a Create Group link in the left navigation column. If you don't find it there, use your Internet browser and go to www.facebook.com/groups.

2. On the Facebook Groups Page, click the Create Groups

button on the top-right side. A pop-up box appears, as shown in Figure 7-9.

3. First, click the down arrow in the corner of the Group Name text box and select from an assortment of unique icons to identify with your Group (the default icon is so boring). This icon will show up on your Home page's navigation links next to the name of your Group.

4. Give your Group a name by typing it in the Group Name text box provided.

5. Add initial members by typing their names in the Members text box. As you type, a drop-down menu will appear, showing matching Facebook friends. Once you see an entry with the correct person's name and photo, click it, and that friend becomes part of your list in the Members box. Continue to type in names until you've invited all the folks you want in the Group.

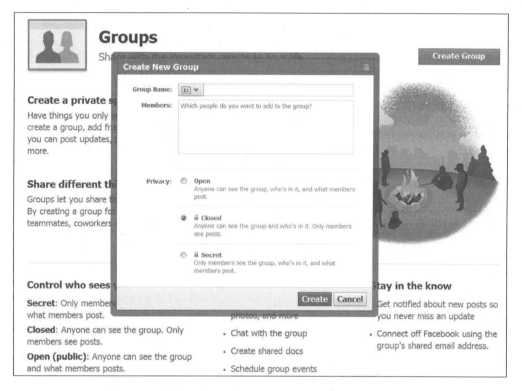

Figure 7-9

6. Select the appropriate option button next to the Privacy setting you want for your Group. You can change your Privacy setting later on if you wish — as long as the total membership of your Group remains under 250.

7. Click the Create Group button when you're finished: Notifications and e-mail messages (similar to the one shown in Figure 7-10) will go out to everyone you've invited. The Group link now shows up on your Home page (in the left column) when you're signed in to Facebook.

Figure 7-10

You will be transported to your brand-spanking-new Group Home page on Facebook.

Customizing Your Group's Look and Feel

Bravo! You've started a Group and you can see a tiny thumbnail of every Facebook friend you've invited in the upper-left side of the Group's Home page. Now it's time to customize the look and feel of your Group's Home page to make it more interesting for the members.

To make modifications to your Page, follow these steps:

1. On the Group page, click the down arrow next to the little Cogwheel icon in the upper-left corner and a menu will appear, as shown in Figure 7-11.

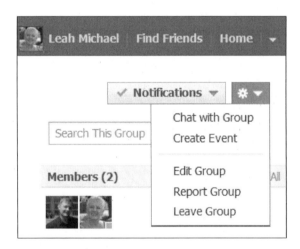

Figure 7-11

2. Click Edit Group, and you'll come to a Page where you can perform several functions:

   ■ **Upload a photo** from your computer for the top of your Group page. If it's a family Group, why not

213

post a photo from a family reunion, or one of your immediate family? A special interest? Post a photo that best identifies your interests.

- **Change the name.** If the name you gave the Group initially doesn't suit your fancy, you can easily change it by typing in a new name in the text box provided.

- **Change the Privacy** of your Group. You can change it from Public to Secret with a click of your mouse!

- **Approve members.** If you want to approve members before they can join (remember that anyone who is a member can invite people), click the box next to Membership Approval so that a check mark appears there.

- **Set up a Group e-mail address.** Click this box to give your Group its own e-mail address. The e-mail address will be whatever name you give it — followed by @groups.facebook.com. The e-mail address will be sent to all members after you click Create Email. Members can then use this address to e-mail posts directly to the Group page.

- **Add a Description.** Give your Group a description or a mission statement.

- **Set Posting Permissions.** Select the option button next to your choice to either allow all members to post to the Group page, or just the administrator. (What fun is that?)

3. After you've made your changes, click Save and your Group page will reflect all your custom settings.

 Should you ever decide to discontinue your Group, you can remove it from Facebook by removing the names of all its members (on the Members section of the Group page). Facebook automatically deletes Groups that have no members.

Chapter 8

Embracing Events, Messaging, and Birthdays

Facebook gives you so many ways to share. It's about connecting, congratulating, and announcing. Through Facebook, you can plan get-togethers — either in person or virtually on video messaging. Facebook will even suggest events that you might want to attend (those open to the public) based on your friends' hobbies and passions.

activities

tech 2 to connect

- Accessing Event Invitations
- Finding Events to Attend
- Accepting Invitations — Or Not
- Declining an Event in Stealth Mode
- Creating Your Own Event
- Using a Private Message to Talk to a Friend
- Finding Out When It's Your Friend's Birthday
- Sending Wishes on Friends' Birthdays

Accessing Event Invitations

It's nice to get invitations to special events, and Facebook allows you and your friends to create events and invite each other to participate. These can be real-life events or virtual ones, where people get together in a chat or to watch a TV show. The sky's the limit. To find out whether you've been invited to an event, you've got several options:

1. Click the Notifications globe icon on the top menu of any Facebook page to find current notifications and invitations from friends.

2. Go to your Home page and click the Events link on the left-side menu (see Figure 8-1) to access upcoming and past events.

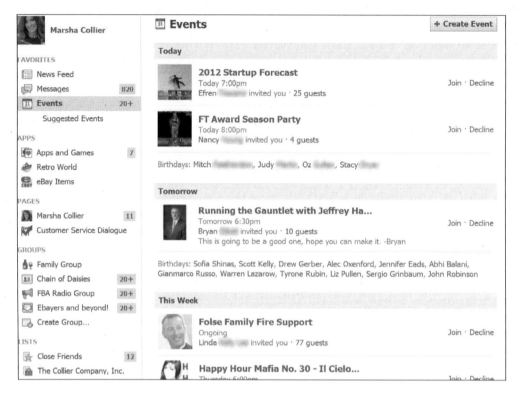

Figure 8-1

3. You can also find upcoming events in the right column of your Home page. Scroll down below the ads and the Ticker to find the link (it's an icon of a page-a-day calendar) and click it. A list will pop out with current invitations, as shown in Figure 8-2.

Figure 8-2

If you have turned on e-mail notifications for the Events application, you will receive an e-mail about any upcoming event. And if you know the name of an upcoming event, you can access an individual event by typing its name into the Search box at the top of your Home page.

4. Facebook will also be glad to text your smartphone with notifications. But do realize that these notifications will be for everything that Facebook considers to be worthy of a notification — which is anything your friends do on Facebook. (If you have a comfortably small group of Facebook friends that you want to keep track of, no problem; if you have a horde, you may want to think twice.) For instructions on how to set up text messaging in the Notifications area of your Account Settings page, visit Chapter 5.

Finding Events to Attend

No invitations? You mean your friends haven't planned a thing? Aside from thinking up something and planning an event yourself, you can find events that Facebook thinks you'd like to attend:

1. Go to your Home page by clicking the word Home at the top of any Facebook page.

2. In the link area on the left side of the Home page, click Events to go to your Events page.

3. On the Events page, next to the Create Event button, you see a magnifying-glass icon with a down arrow next to it.

4. Click the down arrow to reveal a menu with several items. Choose Suggested Events.

5. The resulting Suggested Events page (shown in Figure 8-3) presents you with an interesting array of places to go and people to see. You might just enjoy attending!

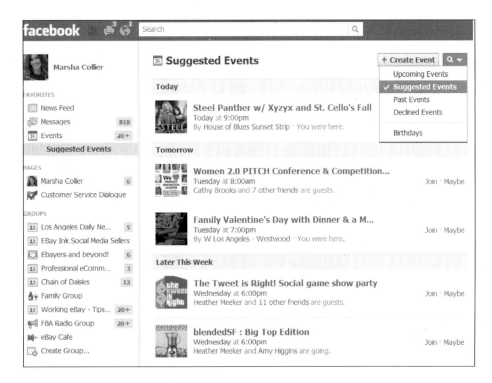

Figure 8-3

Accepting Invitations — Or Not

Now that you know where to look for events, here's how to RSVP:

1. Once you've received an invitation to an event, you can click the event title to get to the Event page.

2. The Event page will have a description of the event. Read it and make your decision as to whether you choose to attend.

3. On the left side of the Page, you will see a list of people who have accepted the invitation, those who responded *Maybe,* those who declined, and those who haven't yet responded.

4. When you've read all the pertinent information, you can RSVP by using the buttons (see Figure 8-4) at the upper-right of the Event page. Click the Join button to say that you'll be there, click Maybe if you're not sure you can make it (this signals the administrator of the event that at least you're interested), and Decline if you can't make it.

Figure 8-4

5. When you click one of the buttons, a window opens and suggests that you post a comment to the Event Wall, as shown in Figure 8-5.

Declining an Event in Stealth Mode

Lots of folks on Facebook get carried away and invite everyone they can imagine to a virtual event. Sometimes they rarely consider whether their invitees will be interested; they just issue a blanket invite.

Sometimes, of course, an event may be based on something you're not comfortable with — perhaps with a particular business, political, charitable, or religious theme. Sometimes I find myself invited to charitable events in distant cities!

You don't want to offend the person who invited you — but you don't want to show up on the list of Declines. What to do? Follow the instructions given here and you'll be removed from the guest list. Odds are (if enough people were invited) the organizer never has to be the wiser.

Here's how to remove your name from the guest list in stealth mode:

1. Click the event's title and go to the corresponding Event page.

2. Find your name under the Invited heading on the left side of the page (Facebook will put your name at the top when you're signed in to the site).

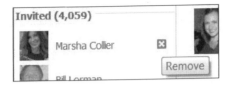

Figure 8-7

3. Hover your mouse pointer (without clicking) over your name: A small *x* will appear to the right and you'll see a pop-up that says *Remove*.

4. Click the *x* and you will be presented with a verification window (as in Figure 8-8). Be sure you want to be removed from the Guest list — and if you do, click Okay.

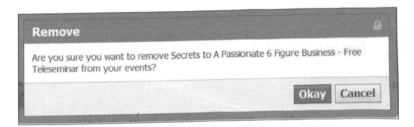

Figure 8-8

5. The dialog box you just clicked will be replaced with one that says *You were successfully removed from the Event.*

Creating Your Own Event

Do you want to invite a select group of your friends over for a Sunday Bar-B-Q? How about inviting everyone you know to meet you at the local theater to watch a movie? Any type of event is up for inviting — and Facebook makes it easy. You can even invite friends who are not members of Facebook. (Maybe they'll see what they're missing and join you in the fun!)

There are two types of events:

- **Invite-Only:** Your friends who have received your invitations are the only ones who can access the Event page. Those who haven't been invited can't find it in public search, either. You can decide whether you want to allow your guests to invite additional friends.

- **Public:** The event is open to the public and will be listed in public search. You have no control over who sees that the event is happening, or who can view the Event page.

Now here's how to create an event of your own:

1. Click the Events link that you find in the left column of your Home page.

2. On the resulting Events page, click Create Event in the upper-right corner (see Figure 8-9).

Figure 8-9

3. On the Create Event page, type a title for your get-together in the Event Name text box. Make the name descriptive and interesting so that when your friends see the invitation, they'll be dying to check it out.

4. Insert the date by clicking the small calendar icon. A calendar opens, and you can navigate to the appropriate date. Click the date and the calendar selector will disappear. Next to the date, let people know what time you want the event to start by clicking the down arrow and choosing the time from the drop-down list.

5. You need to let people know where the event will take place. Type the location in the Location text box. If you want to give the prospective attendees an exact address, click the Add Street Address link and fill in the Street and City text boxes to give these further details. You also have the option to add a map if the location is currently listed in Facebook Places.

6. Give your friends a clue as to what you've planned. Type a cheery description (think "infomercial") in the text box. Your invitation will now look something like the one shown in Figure 8-10.

Create Event

Event Name:	Pre 4th of July Bar-B-Que
Date and Time:	7/1/2012 12:30 pm Add end time
Location:	My House!
	Add street address
Details:	Let's get together for a swim and some wonderful food
Who's Invited:	**Select Guests**

☑ Make this event public (anyone can see and join)
☑ Show the guest list on the event page

Create Event

\+ Add Event Photo

Figure 8-10

7. To select guests, click the Select Guests button. A window will open with pictures and names of all your friends on Facebook. You can select friends by clicking the check box next to each of their pictures, or type in names and select friends one by one.

If some friends you want to invite are not on Facebook, just type their e-mail addresses in the box labeled *Invite by Email address* and click Submit. The recipients will be able to access the Event page on Facebook and RSVP, but won't have access to any other Facebook functionality — unless they join Facebook, of course.

8. On the Invite Friends page, click the link to Add a Personal Message, if you want to add something to the invitations.

9. Once you've made all your invitee selections, click Save and Close, and you return to the Create Event page.

10. Indicate — by clicking the check boxes — whether the event is open to the public, or if you wish to show the

229

guest list on the Event page.

11. Double-check your work (although it is editable once you post the event) and click the Create Event button. Your invitations are sent out from Facebook!

Using a Private Message to Talk to a Friend

There are times when what you want to say is not for public consumption. Or perhaps you'd like to send information to your children without others seeing. There's no need to set up any confusing Privacy Settings. Facebook allows you to send a private message to anyone you're friends with. (You can also send private messages to some Facebook members who are not your friends — but before you can, those folks have to specify this permission in their own settings.)

Go to the Timeline Page of the person to whom you want to send a message and find the Message button (it's at the bottom of the screen, under the Cover picture, as shown in Figure 8-11).

The Message button

Figure 8-11

Click the Message button, and you will be brought to a new page that can be seen only by you and by those to whom you send the message.

A New Message box will appear, showing the To: area with your friend's name already filled in. If you want to add other people to the message, click in the To: text box and start typing your other friends' names. Facebook will suggest names as you type — and when you see the friend(s) you'd like to add, click each name you want to add to the To: list (see Figure 8-12).

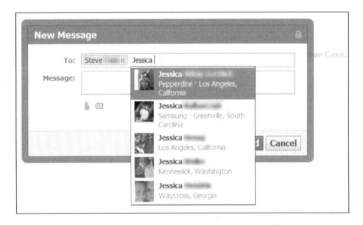

Figure 8-12

Type your message (even letter length) in the text box provided. You can also attach a photo or a link to this message.

When you're satisfied that your message is complete, click Send and a message notification will be sent to your friend(s). (The Message icon on the top of each friend's Facebook Page will also indicate a new message received.)

Finding Out When It's Your Friend's Birthday

If you have no current birthdays in your News Feed, or perhaps you want to play around with astrology, here's how you get to the master list of your Facebook Friends' birthdays:

1. Click Home (in the blue bar at the top right of a Facebook page) to go to your News Feed on your Home page.

2. Click the Events link from the navigation on the left side of the page.

3. Next to the Create Event button, click the small down arrow next to the magnifying glass.

4. Select birthdays by clicking your mouse, and you'll see a page that lists your friends' birthdays (in upcoming date order), as shown in Figure 8-13.

Figure 8-13

233

Sending Wishes on Friends' Birthdays

One of my favorite daily tasks is visiting Facebook and wishing *Happy Birthday* to as many of my friends as possible. You'll get to know how much fun this can be when it's your birthday. Having hundreds of birthday wishes posted on your Wall by friends is pretty amazing. On my last birthday, 498 people wished me happy birthday; the memory of that is archived in my Timeline (shown in Figure 8-14).

Figure 8-14

Although everyone's Facebook Page shows a birthdate (though not necessarily the year), you'll find it almost impossible to keep track of all your friends' birthdays. But

Facebook has a Birthday tool that makes sending wishes easy. Just try these steps:

1. Click the Home link on the top Navigation bar of any Facebook page. Scroll down the page and you see some notifications in the right column, below the ticker.

2. Find the small icon that looks like a gift with a ribbon. If a friend's name appears there, click the name and you arrive at the friend's Page to make a comment.

3. If more than one of your friends has a birthday, the notification will say *And Others*. To leave wishes en masse for your friends, click the And Others link and a window will pop up (refer to Figure 8-15).

Figure 8-15

4. A list of all your friends having birthdays appears, and you can add birthday wishes that will appear on your friends' Pages. Just type your message in the text box next to each friend's name and press Enter when you finish.

5. When your comment is posted, you will see a confirmation that you wrote on someone's Wall.

 If you'd like to go to a page that lists all your friends' birthdays, click the See All link at the top right of the Today's Birthdays list window. This will take you to the Events: Birthdays page, which lists all upcoming birthdays of your friends.

Chapter 9

Playing Around with Facebook Games and Apps

The social component of Facebook goes far beyond sharing pictures and comments. You'll find (and no doubt hear in the news) about the varied ways you can play games with other people on Facebook. The words *apps* (applications) and *games* are tossed around interchangeably. When you're on the Facebook platform, they're very much the

activities

tech 2 connect

- Finding Games and Apps
- Finding a Specific Game or App
- Giving Permissions to Join
- Controlling App Privacy or Opting Out
- Video-Calling through Facebook Chat
- Playing Music with Your Friends

same — because a game *is* an application.

In this chapter, I show you how to find games and apps, as well as how to manage your interaction with them. I also introduce you to a couple of specific apps that offer another means for connecting with friends through video-calling and enjoying music together.

Finding Games and Apps

With the wealth of apps and games Facebook has available, finding a game that you'll enjoy playing or an app that's useful can be a challenge. You can rely on recommendations from your Facebook friends or try this:

1. Click the Home link in the upper-right corner of any Facebook page to go your Home page.

2. In the left navigation column of your Home page, click the Apps and Games link, as shown in Figure 9-1.

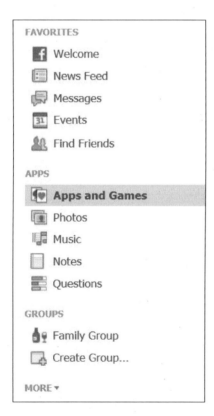

Figure 9-1

3. You will arrive at the Apps and Games hub page, which has several views that change depending on your Facebook usage. You can look through these views to see some of the apps and games that are available:

- **Recommended Games and Recommended Apps.** If you're new to games and apps, Recommended Games will be your opening view (see Figure 9-2). According to Facebook, the list is compiled by looking at the top games on Facebook with more than 100,000 monthly active users and giving priority to those games with the highest user satisfaction scores. (Sounds good to me!)

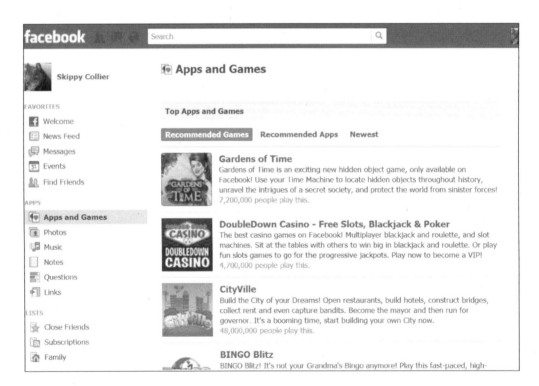

Figure 9-2

Newest. This is a listing of the newest apps and games as they appear on Facebook. I'm more of a tried-and-true kind of person, so I pass these by and go for recommendations instead.

Friends Using. If friends have played an online game, this activity will appear at the top of the page.

In multi-player games, it's probably more fun to play with people you know. The apps and games will be listed here, along with the names of friends using them.

Invites from Friends. If you have already established friends on Facebook, you may also see this category. If you do, a friend has recommended that you join an online game. Such requests will appear at the top of the page after you click Invites from Friends, as shown in Figure 9-3.

You may also see "Featured" or "Discover New Games" on the far right of the page. These selections currently include the apps and games that may be testing Facebook Credits (a new feature on Facebook). Facebook says the selection process for the Games Dashboard will likely evolve over time.

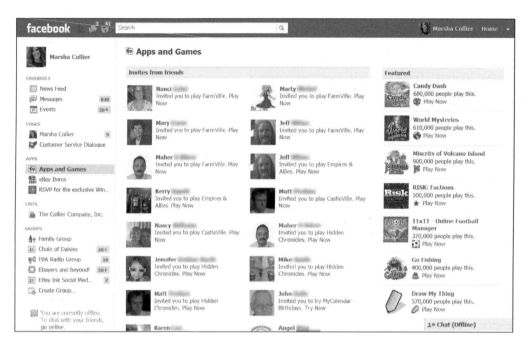

Figure 9-3

Finding a Specific Game or App

If you've heard about a particular game from friends or in the news media and you'd like to check it out, you can search on the Apps and Games hub page just as you'd perform any search on Facebook. Follow these steps:

1. In the Search box at the top of the Apps and Games hub page, type the name of the game or app you're looking for.

2. A list of the top results will appear. You'll notice that my search for *Words with Friends* appeared twice in my results — listed once under the game itself and again as a Page for the app.

Figure 9-4

3. To find out more about a game you searched for, click the link to the app's page. Usually, you arrive at a gated page (see Figure 9-5) that requests you to "Like" or "Play" immediately — but hold on. Check out the page's left-side navigation links: You have options to click Info (and find out more about the game) or Wall (and see postings about the game).

Figure 9-5

4. Click each link so you can read the information and postings. That way you get an idea of what's in store if and when you decide you want to play the game.

5. If you decide to give the game a try, click the Play or Play the Game link (this wording varies from app to app), and you're in!

Giving Permissions to Join

When you find a game or app you're interested in, joining in requires you to give the application certain permissions when it comes to your Facebook account. All apps will want access to your name, Profile picture, gender, username, networks, user ID (account number), and just about anything on your Profile that you've made public. They also have access to your Friends list.

Some apps will want very little; others want more access to your information. Figure 9-6 shows you some common requests.

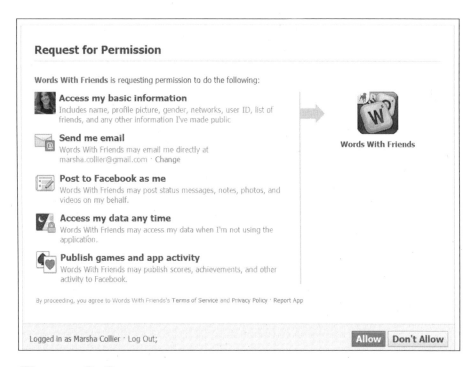

Figure 9-6

Confusing? Perhaps. Here are some simplified definitions of requests for permissions that you may encounter:

- **Access my basic information:** Allows the game or app to see anything you've publicly posted on Facebook about yourself, including your name, gender, age, Profile pictures, username, and networks.

- **Access my Profile information:** Includes Groups you've joined and Pages you've Liked. Also, apps can see the info in sections such as Music, TV, Movies, Books, Quotes, About Me, Activities, Interests, Groups, Events, Notes, Birthday, Hometown, Current City, Website, Religious and Political Views, Education History, Work History, and Facebook Status.

- **Access my family & relationships:** Lets apps and games see whom you've publicly named as your Significant Other or other Relationship Details, your Family Members you've publicly connected with, and Relationship Status.

- **Send me email:** Sends you e-mails about the app or game.

- **Post to Facebook as me:** When you reach a certain level of gameplay, you may want that information to be posted to your Wall. The app will do that with your permission.

- **Access my data at any time:** The app may go online at any time and review your data. (I usually opt out of this review — see the next section in this chapter for how to do this.)

- **Publish games and app activity:** Publish activity to your Wall.

- **Access information people share with me:** If your friends have shared the following information about themselves, it will be available to the app: Birthdays, Religious and Political Views, Family Members and Relationship Statuses, Significant Others and Relationship Details, Hometowns, Current Cities, Likes, Music, TV, Movies, Books, Quotes, Activities, Interests, Education History, Work History, Online Presence, Websites, Groups, Events, Notes, Photos, Videos, About Me Details, and Facebook Statuses.

Not all apps and games are equally intrusive. FarmVille (for example) asks only two permissions (in Figure 9-7), and Retro World (see Figure 9-8) goes even more basic with requests.

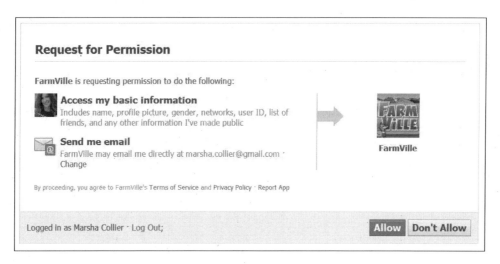

Figure 9-7

Figure 9-8

No Facebook app can post to your Timeline without your permission. Figure 9-8 shows how you can change the Who Can See Activity from This App on Facebook drop-down list to Only Me.

My favorite app?

An app I highly recommend (once you've built up a nice community of friends) on Facebook is Intel The Museum of Me. It accesses your photos, your friends, and your posts and builds a museum exhibit of your activity on Facebook. The Museum of Me is an application that displays information from your Facebook account as viewable "exhibits" in a virtual museum of your very own. It's really fascinating. Search the app or go directly to www.intel.com/museumofme/.

Controlling App Privacy or Opting Out

It would behoove you to go to your Apps Settings every once in a while to double-check that the apps are all playing fair.

To manage your Apps Settings, follow these steps:

1. Click the down arrow next to Home in the upper-right corner of any Facebook page and choose Account Settings from the drop-down menu.

2. Click the Apps link in the left column on the resulting page. A list of all the apps you've joined will appear, as shown in Figure 9-9.

Figure 9-9

3. If you want to remove an app, click the X at the right end of the app's line (next to the Edit link).

4. To select an app and check the permissions you've granted, click the app's name or the Edit link. A list of

250

the active permissions appears below the app's line.

5. To remove any optional permission you don't want, click the associated Remove link.

6. Choose an audience with the drop-down audience-selector list from the App Activity Privacy section, as shown in Figure 9-10. The app can show posts and app activity only to people within the audience you choose.

7. After you complete your changes, click the Save button at the bottom of the window.

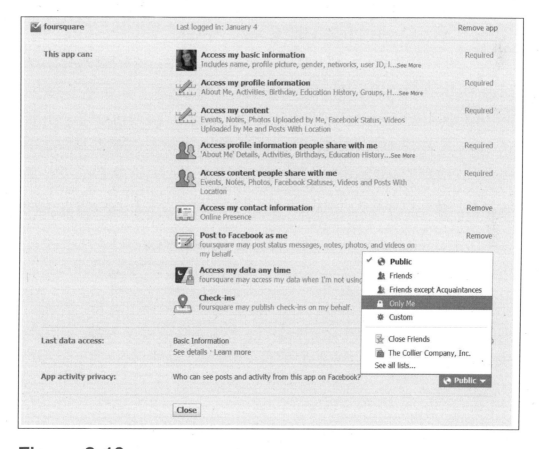

Figure 9-10

To find out how to manage your General Settings for apps and websites, please refer to Chapter 5.

If you find that an app you're using (or that one of your friends is using) clogs up your News Feed or Wall with postings you'd rather not see, you can remove it forever (or just temporarily). Just do this:

1. Find a post sent from the offending app.

2. Mouse over the title of the post, and an icon will appear in the right corner.

3. After you click the icon, a menu will appear (as shown in Figure 9-11) with options for dealing with the post or the app itself.

4. Select Hide all Recent *Name of App* Activity from Timeline, and you will never see posts from that app again.

5. To remove a single post, select Remove *App Name*.

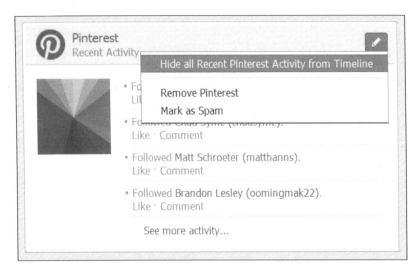

Figure 9-11

Video-Calling through Facebook Chat

Facebook Chat can be a lot of fun, but the chatting feature really boils down to sending text messages back and forth with your friends. As I mention in Chapter 4, wouldn't you prefer to actually see your friends and chat face to face? In these days of reality TV and cameras in almost every phone, the need to get all gussied up for the camera is passé. On a personal note, I have discovered that the cameras built into computers these days are very forgiving. I think this may have something to do with the light balance? Whatever the technical reason is, the forgiving nature makes me much more open to turning on my computer's camera for a call. Take it from me; I'm sure I am one of the last holdouts.

When you make a video call, not only can your friends and family see you, but you also get to see them! Real live video is much more fulfilling than viewing static pictures on a webpage or snapshots in an album. The only requirement for seeing each other through Facebook is that both parties have webcams and microphones.

 If your friends have a video camera on their computers — and you don't — don't worry. You will still be able to see and hear your friends during a video chat.

So give it a try:

1. In the bottom-right corner of every Facebook page is your Chat box. If it's not open, click the word *Chat,* and

253

a list (with Profile photos) of your online friends will appear.

 If you don't see the friend you're looking for in the Chat list, type his or her name in the Search box at the bottom. A list of friends' names matching the name you type will appear.

2. If your friend is online and available to chat, you'll see a green button next to his or her name. Double-click the name, and a Chat window will open.

3. Click the icon that looks like a tiny video camera in the Chat box next to your friend's name (as in Figure 9-12) to initiate a video chat. If you don't see the little camera, your friend may not be online to chat.

Figure 9-12

4. If you have never used video chat through Facebook before, you will have to set up the software that enables Facebook to use Skype to make the call. A window will pop up (see Figure 9-13), notifying you that you must complete a one-time setup. (After setup is complete, you are ready to have fun with your first call.)

Figure 9-13

5. In the Set Up Video Calling window, click the Install button. Facebook will download a file to your computer. Click Keep to set up video calling.

6. If you have a computer running Windows, you will see a Security Warning dialog box from your system; the warning asks approval to run the setup software. Doing so is perfectly safe; just click the Run button.

7. After you set up the software, you'll be able to click the little video camera icon to initiate a video chat. A window will pop-up, saying that Facebook is contacting your friend, as shown in Figure 9-14.

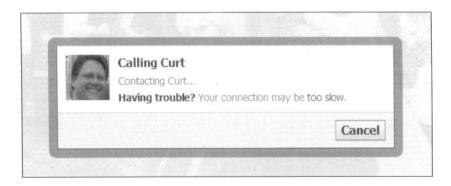

Figure 9-14

8. After your friend answers the call to chat, you will see your friend in a large window, and a postage-size video window of you will appear in the corner.

Now that you are set up for video calling, you can go to any friend's Facebook Page to call him or her directly. Click the small Cogwheel icon under your friend's Cover photo to reveal a contact menu. Select Call from the menu (see Figure 9-15), and Facebook will initiate your video chat.

Figure 9-15

9. To end your video call, just close the video window.

Playing Music with Your Friends

Remember how much fun playing records with friends was in the days of vinyl? When you and your friends could play your favorite music for each other? You can do that again on Facebook with the help of any number of applications. Use the information in this chapter's first two sections to find a music app, or follow these steps:

1. Click Home in the upper-right corner of any Facebook page to access your News Feed. You may see a friend "listening" to music, as shown in Figure 9-16.

Figure 9-16

2. Click the Play button, and an app window will open.

3. If you want to listen too, you will have to allow an app permission to run within your Facebook page. Set the Privacy Setting from the drop-down menu on the About This App page by clicking the down arrow on the Public button and selecting your audience.

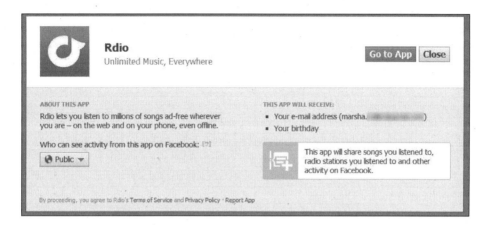

Figure 9-17

4. After you set permissions, click the Go to App button and approve it on the app's page.

Index

Symbols and Numerics

P

About the Author

Marsha Collier spends a good deal of time online. As a blogger, author of the best-selling *For Dummies* books about eBay, and radio host, she shares her love of the online world with millions.

Before her eBay career took off, Marsha owned and operated her own marketing and advertising firm, a company that won numerous awards and earned her "Small Business of the Year" accolades from several organizations. She got started online during the Internet's early years and quickly mastered the art of making friends online.

Marsha is one of the foremost eBay experts and educators in the world and the top-selling eBay author. In 1999, Marsha created the first edition of *eBay For Dummies,* the bestselling book for eBay beginners. She followed up that success with *Starting an eBay Business For Dummies,* a book targeting individuals interested in making e-commerce their full-time profession. Marsha updates these books regularly to keep up with site and market changes.

Marsha's books have sold over 1,000,000 copies (including the special editions in foreign countries — two in Australia, two in Canada, and two in the United Kingdom — as well as translations in Spanish, French, Italian, Chinese, and German).

Along with her writing, Marsha is an experienced e-commerce and customer service educator speaking at conferences all over the world. Embracing social media has earned Marsha awards as an influencer:

- 2011 Forbes: Top 10 Women Social Media Influencers

- 2012 Forbes: Top 50 Social Media Power Influencers

- 2009: 140 Characters Conference NOW Award Winner

- 2012 The 100 Most Powerful Women On Twitter

- 2011 One of Top 10 LA Tech & Twitter Voices in the Los Angeles Tech Scene by Ranker.com

- 2011 PeerIndex #1 Customer Experience Online Influencers

- 2011 #1 Most Influential in Customer Service Mind-Touch

She hosts Computer & Technology Radio on iTunes and the web at www.computerandtechnologyradio.com. Marsha currently resides in Los Angeles, CA. She can be reached via her website at www.marshacollier.com.

The employees of Thorndike Press hope you have enjoyed this Large Print book. All our Thorndike and Wheeler Large Print titles are designed for easy reading, and all our books are made to last. Other Thorndike Press Large Print books are available at your library, through selected bookstores, or directly from us.

For information about titles, please call:

(800) 223-1244

or visit our Web site at:

www.gale.com/thorndike
www.gale.com/wheeler

To share your comments, please write:

Publisher
Thorndike Press
10 Water St., Ste. 310
Waterville, ME 04901